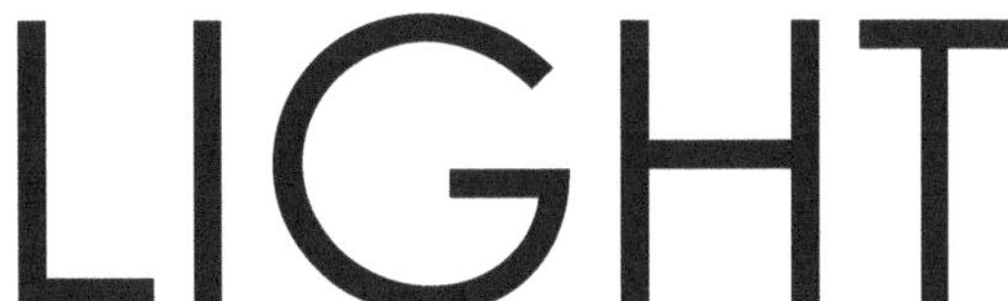

TO

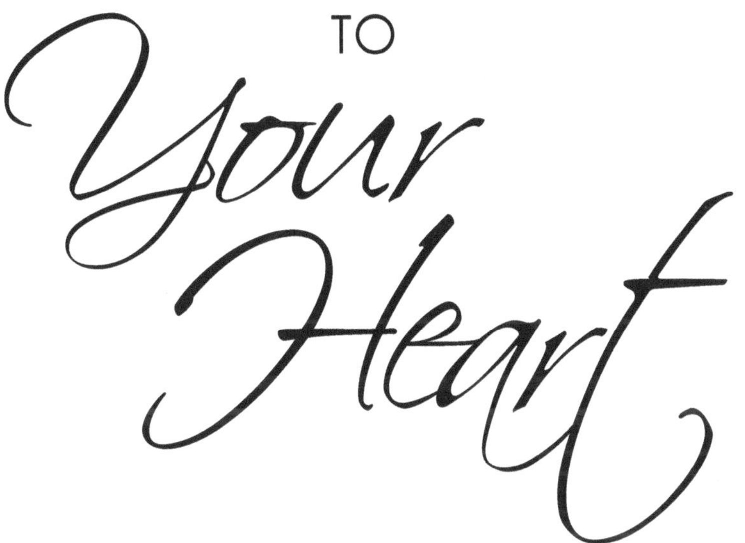

Daily Inspiration for 31 Days

Linda Hayes

Light to Your Heart

Daily Inspiration for 31 Days

Photographs by Linda Hayes

ISBN 978-0-9885453-5-9
Published by Publishing USA www.Publishing-USA.com

Dedication

This daily inspirational book is dedicated to all people seeking light, peace, and joy in their lives. My heartfelt intention is to jumpstart your day with beautiful photographs, insightful words, and affirmations to fill your heart with joy.

I have traveled the world capturing special moments in time with my camera and paired them with words from my heart. May they inspire you to soar like an eagle and share your special light with the world.

I present this new work to my family and friends to inspire them with the beauty of each day. My desire is to share a part of my spirit with them in printed form. Let it encourage them to follow their dreams and walk proudly into their destiny.

"When you are inspired by some great purpose, some extraordinary project, all your thoughts break their bonds: Your mind transcends limitations…and you discover yourself to be a person far greater than you ever dreamed yourself to be."

—Patanjali (Yoga Sutras of Patanjali, 1st-3rd Century, BC)

Introduction

Four years ago I released my first book, ***The Voice Hidden Within Me—A Journey of Discovery and Healing Your Heart***. I shared my most personal life stories, experiences, and life lessons. My deep-rooted inner fears and false beliefs were exposed and dispelled. Healing and self-love came.

Each life chapter brings endings, new beginnings, and a renewed passion for life. We are not the labels we use to identify ourselves. We are the beautiful beings inside our hearts with the power to love and attract what we need. Like attracts like is the Law of Attraction. The Law of Attraction is the Law of Love. Use this law to attract love to yourself and others and bring all good things to you.

I am often asked why my two published books are so different. The first is a transformational self-help book and the second is a cookbook. I now realize that my artistic endeavors are a reflection of who I am. What do I mean by that? I reflect my wide variety of interests and things I love in what I write and photograph. Each book and photo reflects a facet of my life or something I am passionate about. I encourage you to express yourself according to who you are. Don't feel you must conform to a pattern or a mold unless you want to. Just be yourself.

My new book is a compilation of places and things that inspire me and words that sooth my soul. I present to you the world I see through the eye of my camera and the thoughts coming from my spirit. There are 31 photographs paired with 31 inspirational quotes in this book. Enjoy the pictures, quotes, affirmations, and thoughts. Look deeply at the images reflecting a special moment in time.

To gain the most from this book try these suggestions. Read one quote and view its photograph each day for one month. Use the comments and affirmations in your daily activities. You don't have to choose a quote in any particular order. Find the one that calls to you. You may repeat a daily quote for multiple days if you like. Meditate on the inspirational words, reflect, and apply their meanings to your life. Declare the affirmation often. You may find it helpful to write down your thoughts, lessons, and experiences at the end of the day.

May your journey to greatness be an amazing ride full of love, joy, and peace. Color your world with your passion. Fill it with your love and light.

Namaste.

Contents

Part I

Be Present

Every day is a new beginning…

Today will be amazing!

You have 24 hours, 1,440 minutes, 86,400 seconds in a day. You may greet each day with gratitude or dismay. Challenge yourself to make each day an amazing adventure full of new opportunities. Each day gives you another chance to get it right, send out light, and share your spirit with others.

Daily Affirmation

Today is amazing. I have endless opportunities to explore.

Tranquil Dawn 2017
Joshua Tree, CA

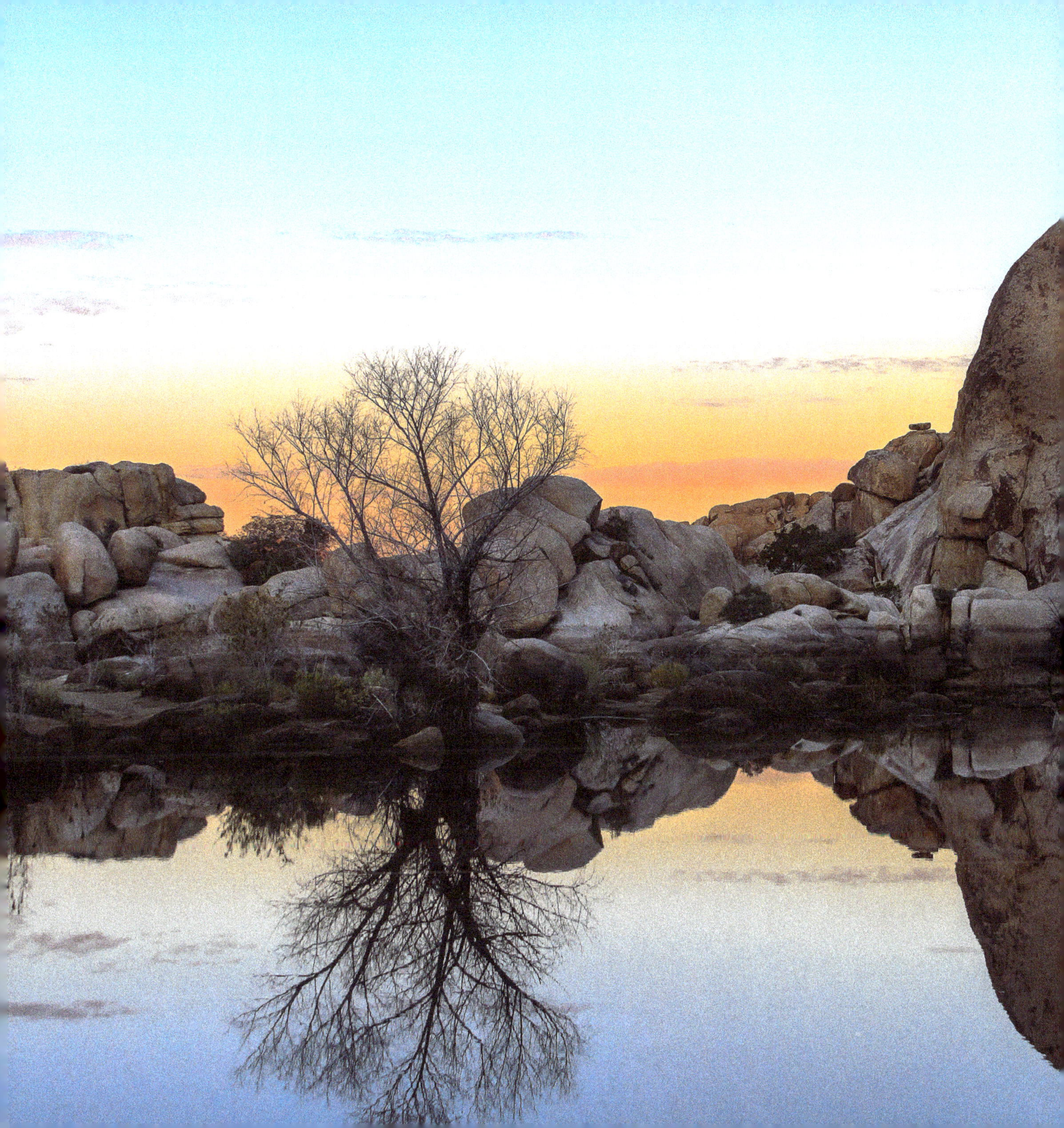

In the early morning light...

I find my peace!

A new day unfolds as the sun rises and its golden light embraces you. Allow time to renew yourself in the calmness of the morning. A new day, your mind clear, a quiet spirit will move you through this day. Loudly declare gratitude and peace from your heart.

Daily Affirmation

Today I am grateful, thankful, and peaceful.

Morning Peace 2016
Lake Havasu, AZ

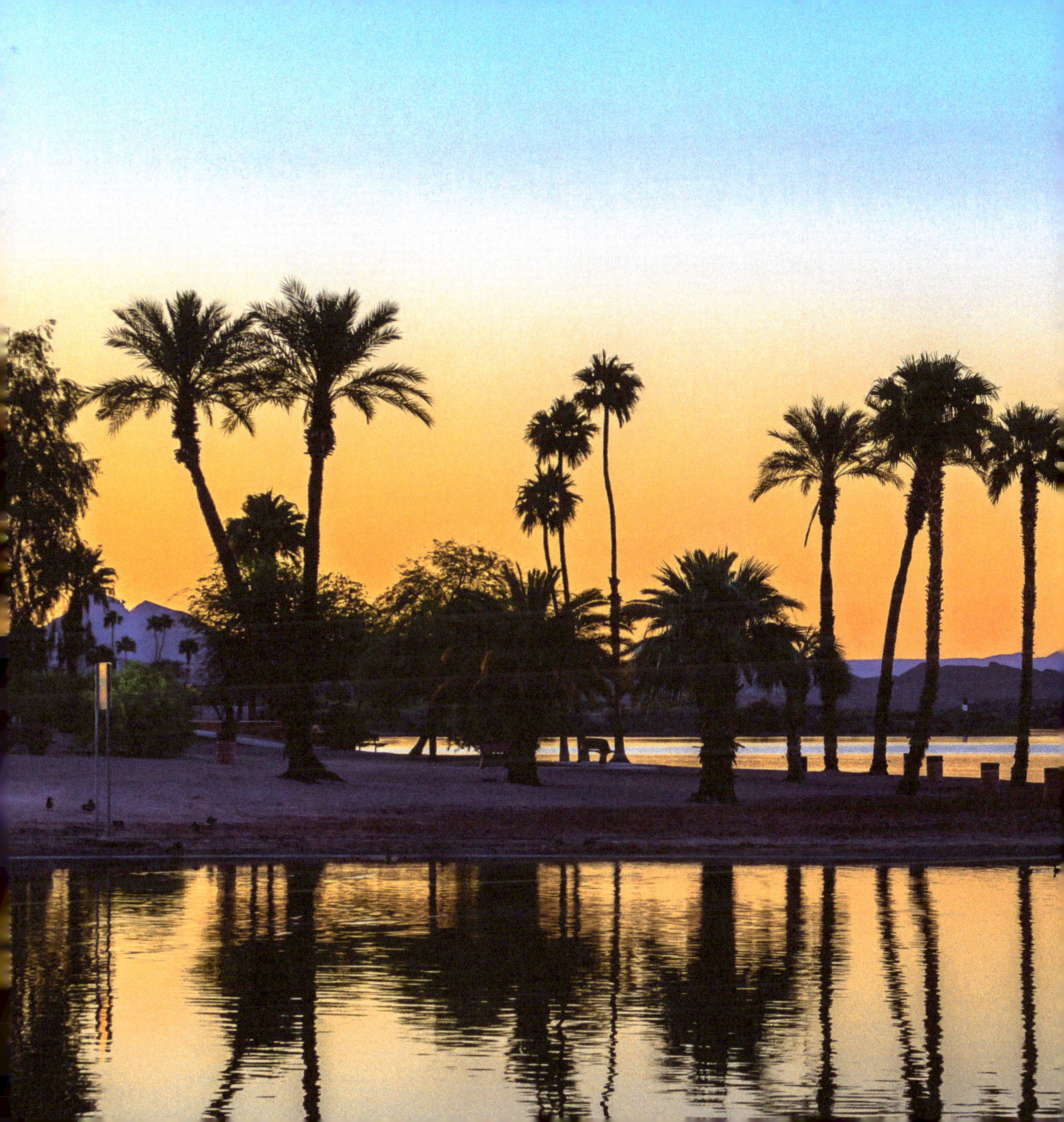

Today's Prayer…

May you be well, may you be peaceful,

may you be happy, may you be loved!

Each day send your healing light with the joyful prayer or mantra above. Send it to yourself to center your heart. Send it to loved ones, your acquaintances, people in conflict with you, and the whole world. Recite this prayer separately for each group as you send them your healing light.

Daily Affirmation

Today I am healthy, happy, peaceful, and loved.

Peaceful Harmony 2016
San Diego, CA

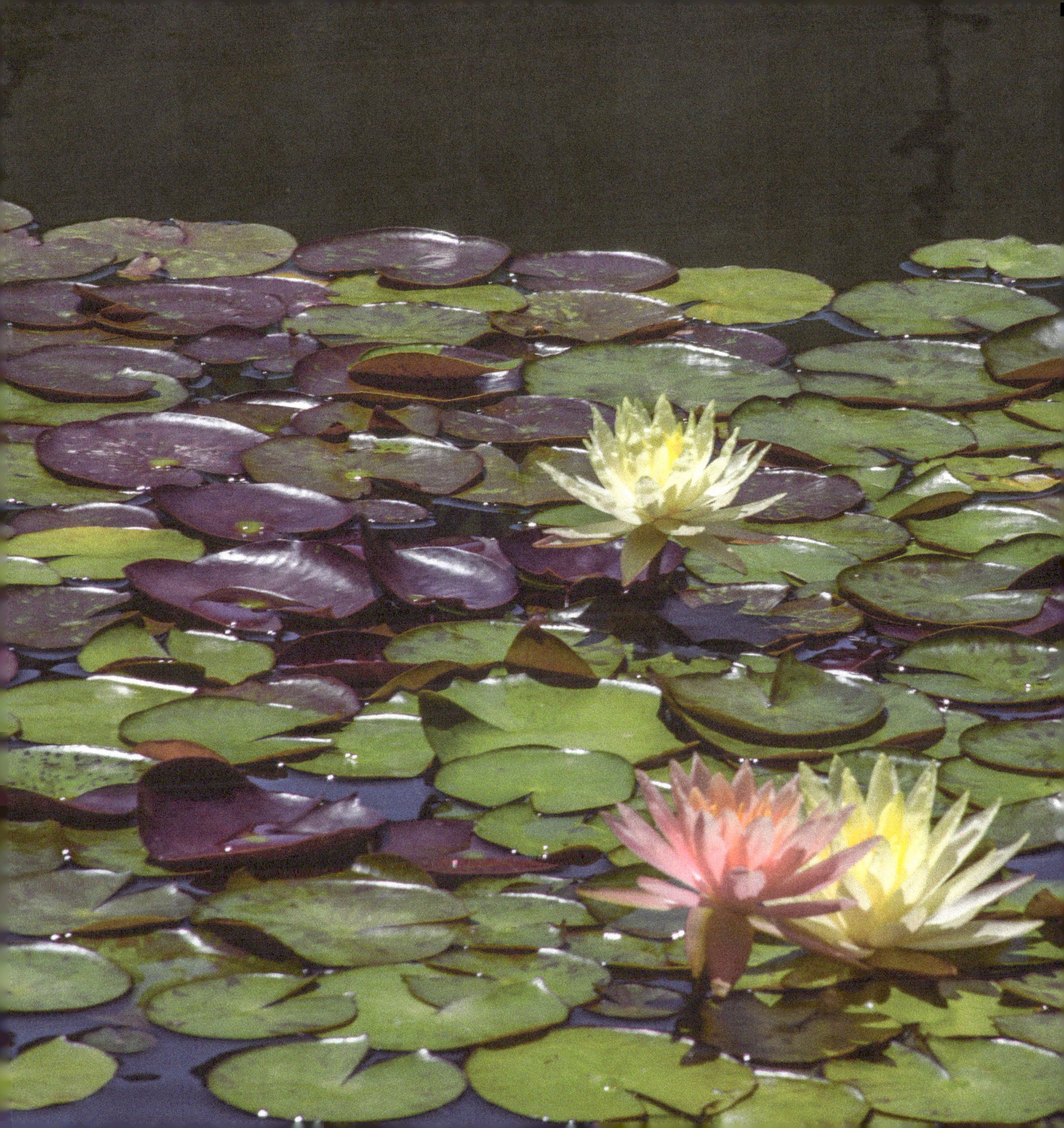

Each moment is a gift...

Stop, observe, and enjoy it!

Practice living in the moment. Unclutter your mind from the bombardment of thoughts and concern about yesterday or tomorrow. Grab the joy from experiencing and cherishing what is in front and around you right now. Mindfully practice living in the present.

Daily Affirmation

Today I embrace this moment. I cherish and accept this gift.

Cherish 2014
San Marino, CA

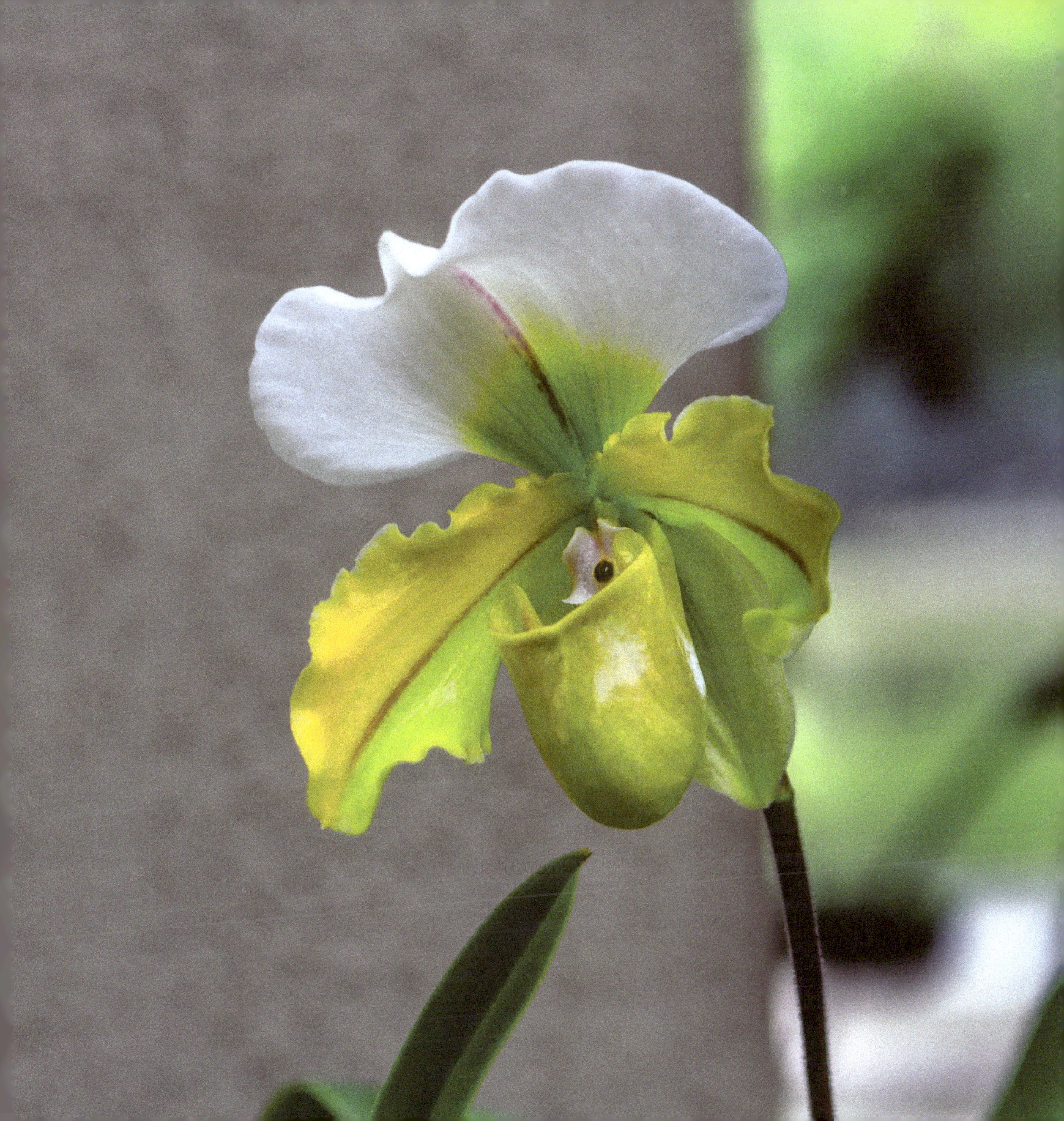

Pause, breathe and relax...

Embrace each moment eagerly!

A person has between 35-48 thoughts per minute or 50,000-70,000 per day. They may become a worrisome partner who talks incessantly. A preoccupied mind doesn't see the moment. Slow down, take a few deep cleansing breaths, and relax. Be present and experience each moment.

Daily Affirmation

Today I quiet my mind. I eagerly embrace NOW.

Quiet Beauty 2016
La Canada, CA

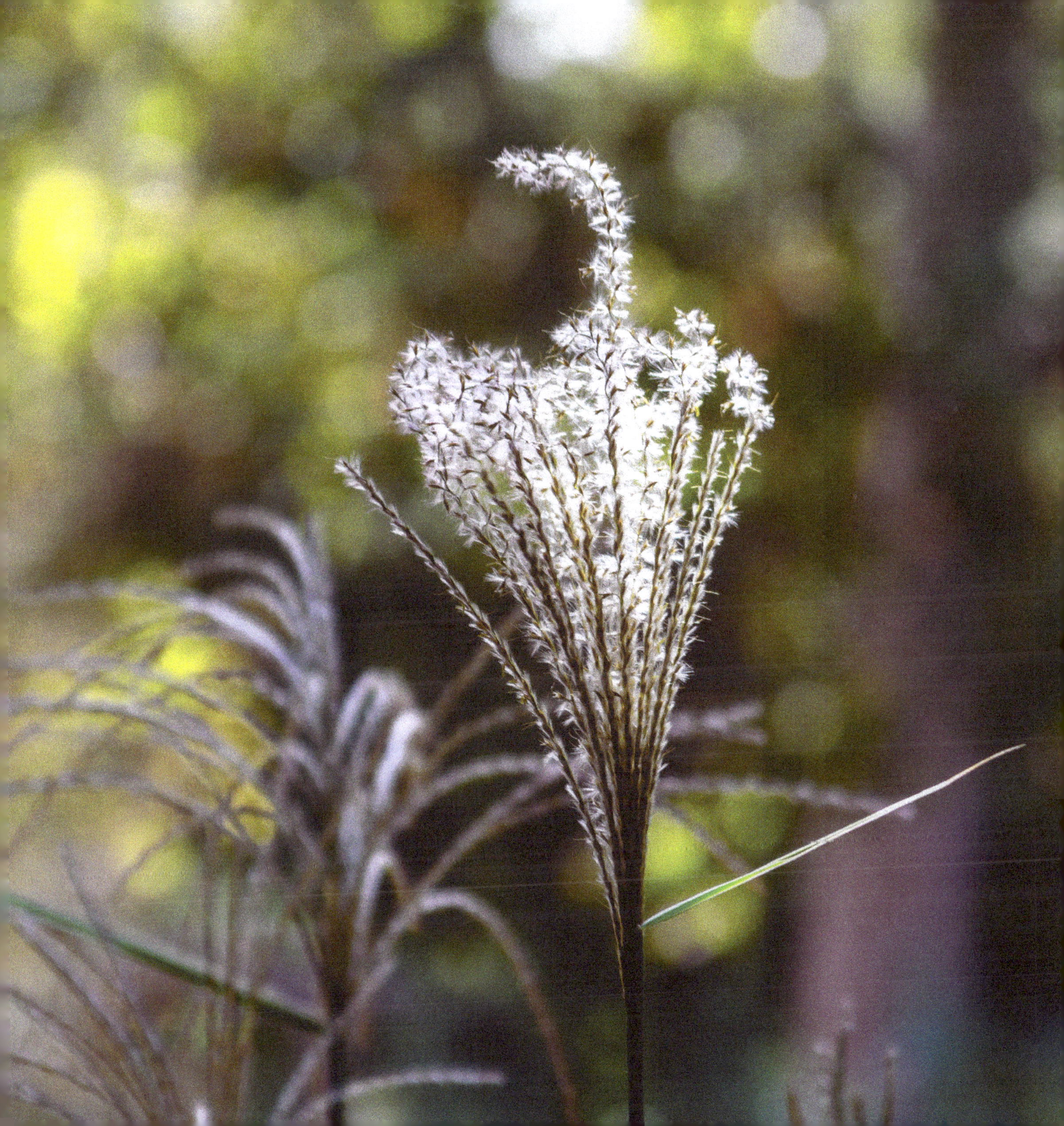

At the end of the day…

Be grateful and content!

Each day is an amazing experience. Problems may manifest and become life lessons. Life lessons teach you how to do it better next time. Stay positive and be grateful. Make a daily mental or actual list of everything you are grateful for in your life. Feel the contentment created by a grateful heart.

Daily Affirmation

Today I am positive, grateful, and content.

Sunrise Sonata 2016
Sedona, AZ

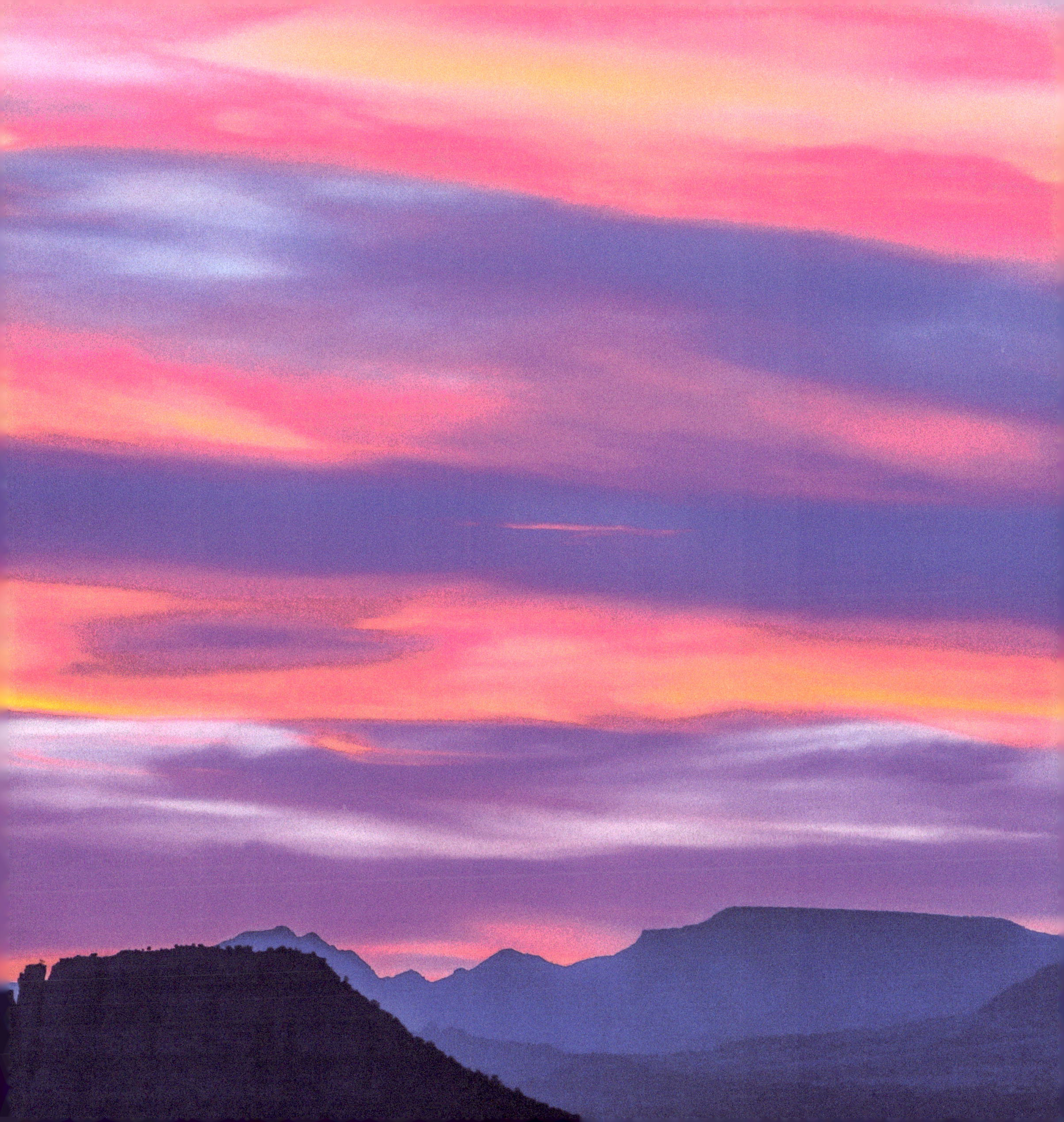

Part II

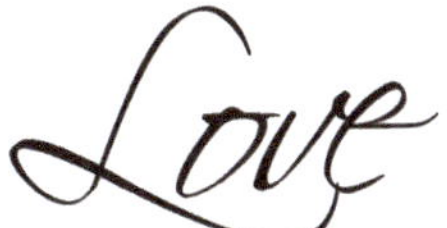

Look inside and see…

The beauty of who you are!

Look at yourself with an eye of discernment. What do you see? Is it the true reflection of the person of your heart or self-imposed opinions of others? Don't devalue your beauty. Embrace your positive qualities. Applaud your inner spirit and beauty. Love yourself and the person of your heart.

Daily Affirmation

I am beautiful and amazing.

Inner Beauty 2016
La Canada, CA

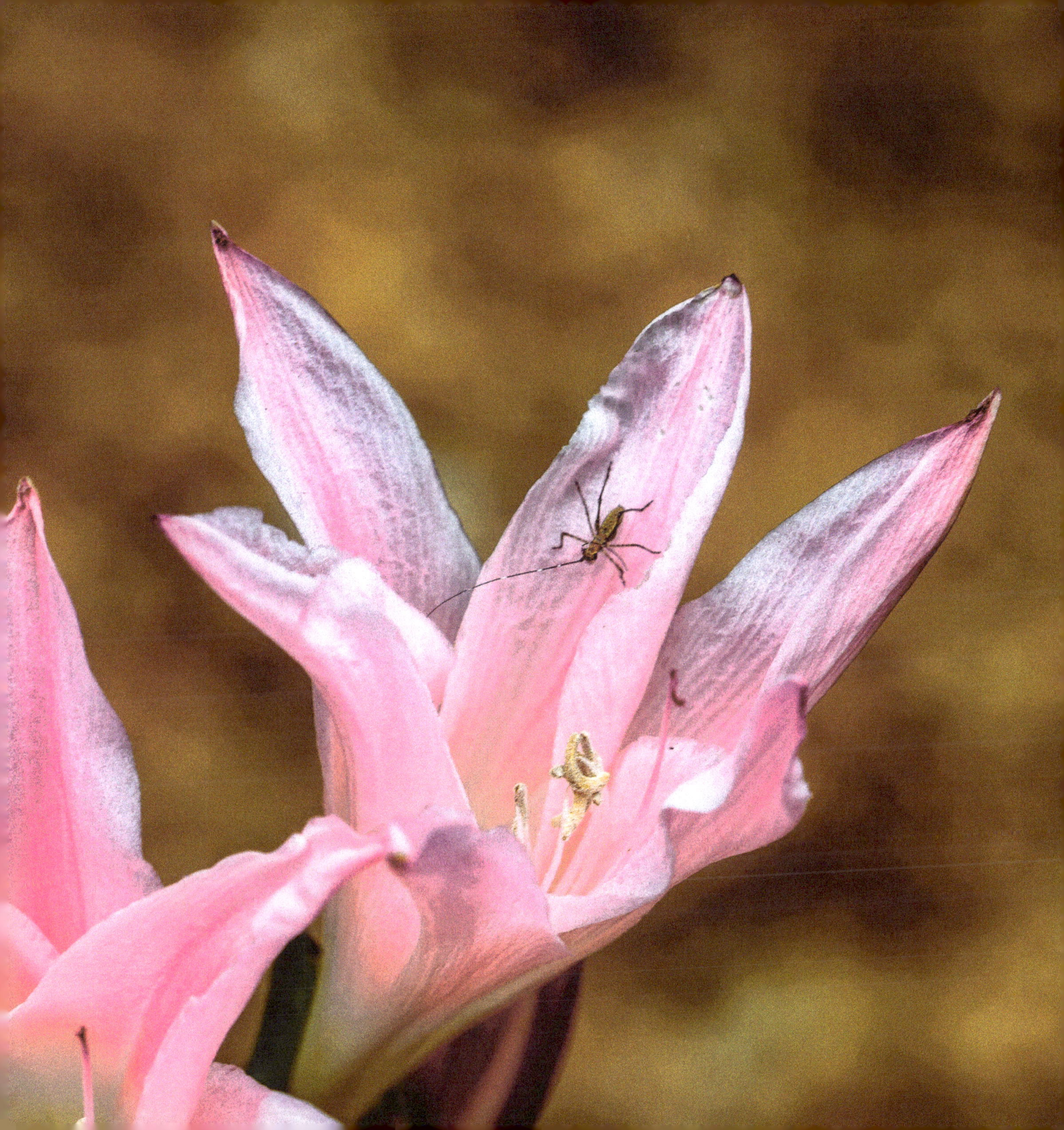

Love who you are…

Share your love with others!

You must love yourself before you can love anyone else. Self-love is the foundation and starting point of all love connections. Accept your accomplishments and failures then turn them into life lessons. Hug yourself. Look into a mirror, look deeply into your eyes, and proclaim your beauty and greatness.

Daily Affirmation

I love who I am. I send my love to the world.

Love Song 2015
San Marino, CA

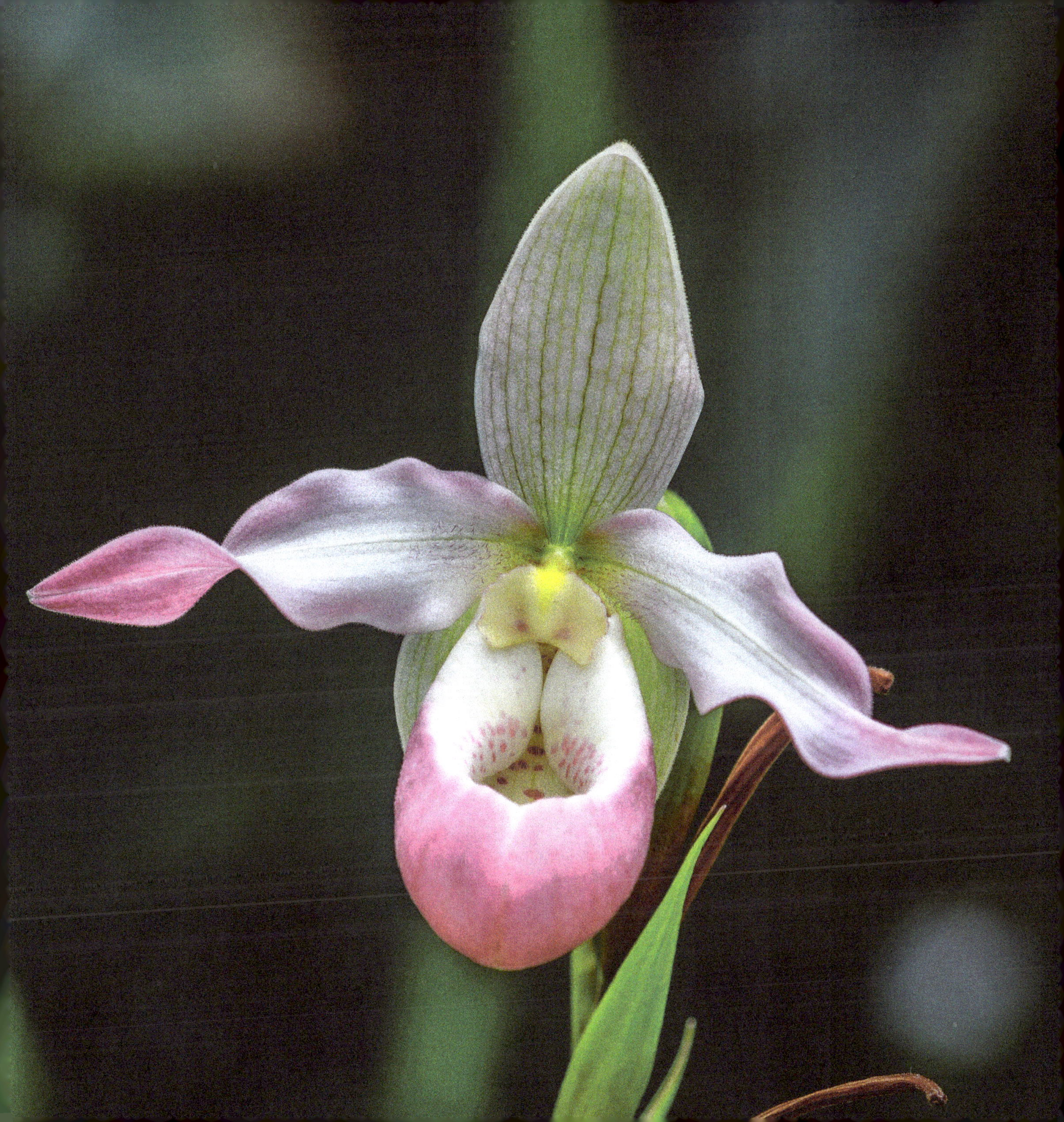

The heart is the center of love

Love's power can change the world!

Your heart center creates love, compassion, kindness, self-love, joy, and generosity. Keep your heart open to allow these beautiful spiritual qualities to flow abundantly. When your heart is open you inspire love and compassion in others. Cultivate the path of the heart.

Daily Affirmation

I open my heart and share it with others.

Heart Center 2016
Encinitas, CA

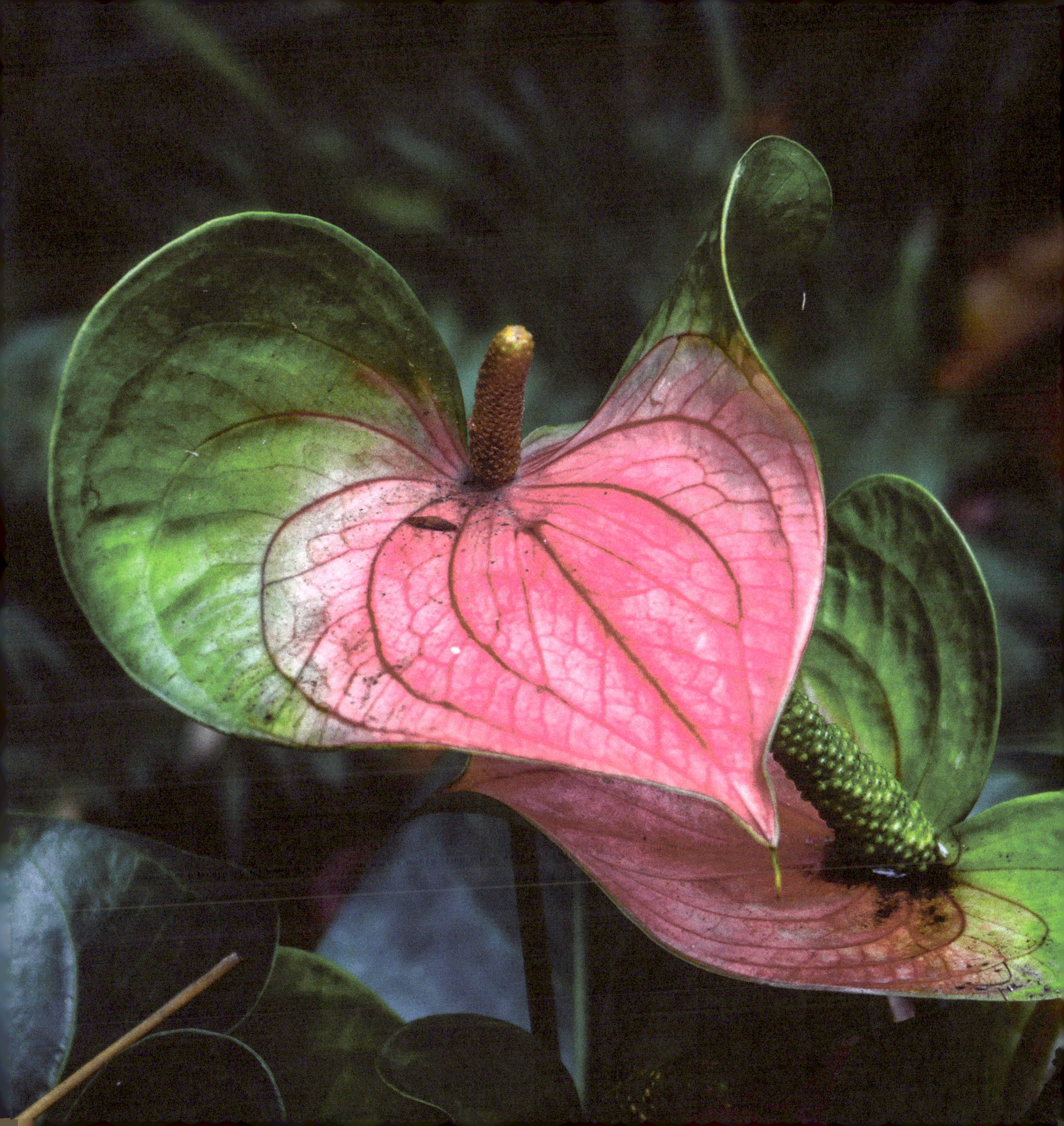

Let's change the world with...

A smile, a word, with love!

You don't know what the simplest act of kindness means to another person. A kind word to a stranger may be all that is needed to brighten their day. Make it a point to share a smile, friendly hello, or kind act everywhere you go.

Daily Affirmation

I share my light with a smile and kindness.

Sharing Grace 2014
Cabo San Lucas, Mexico

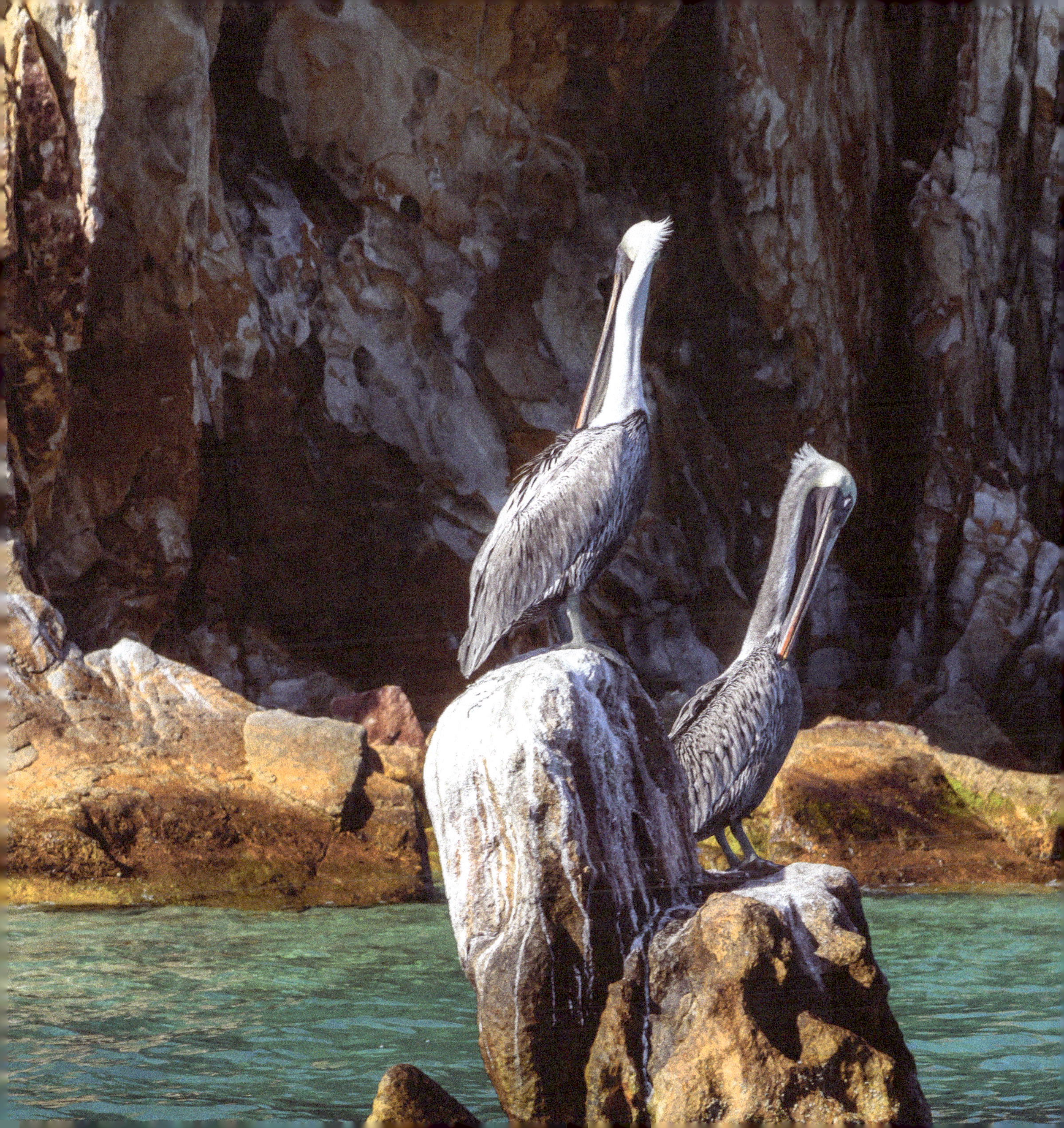

I am happy…

Love and joy inspire me!

When you are happy everything falls into place. The world is bright and wondrous. You are inspired and unstoppable. Don't let negativity cloud your heart. Stay happy and think happy thoughts. Create a happy list with places and experiences that make you feel good. Use it when you need a mood boost.

Daily Affirmation

I am happy. I am inspired.

Happiness 2016
San Marino, CA

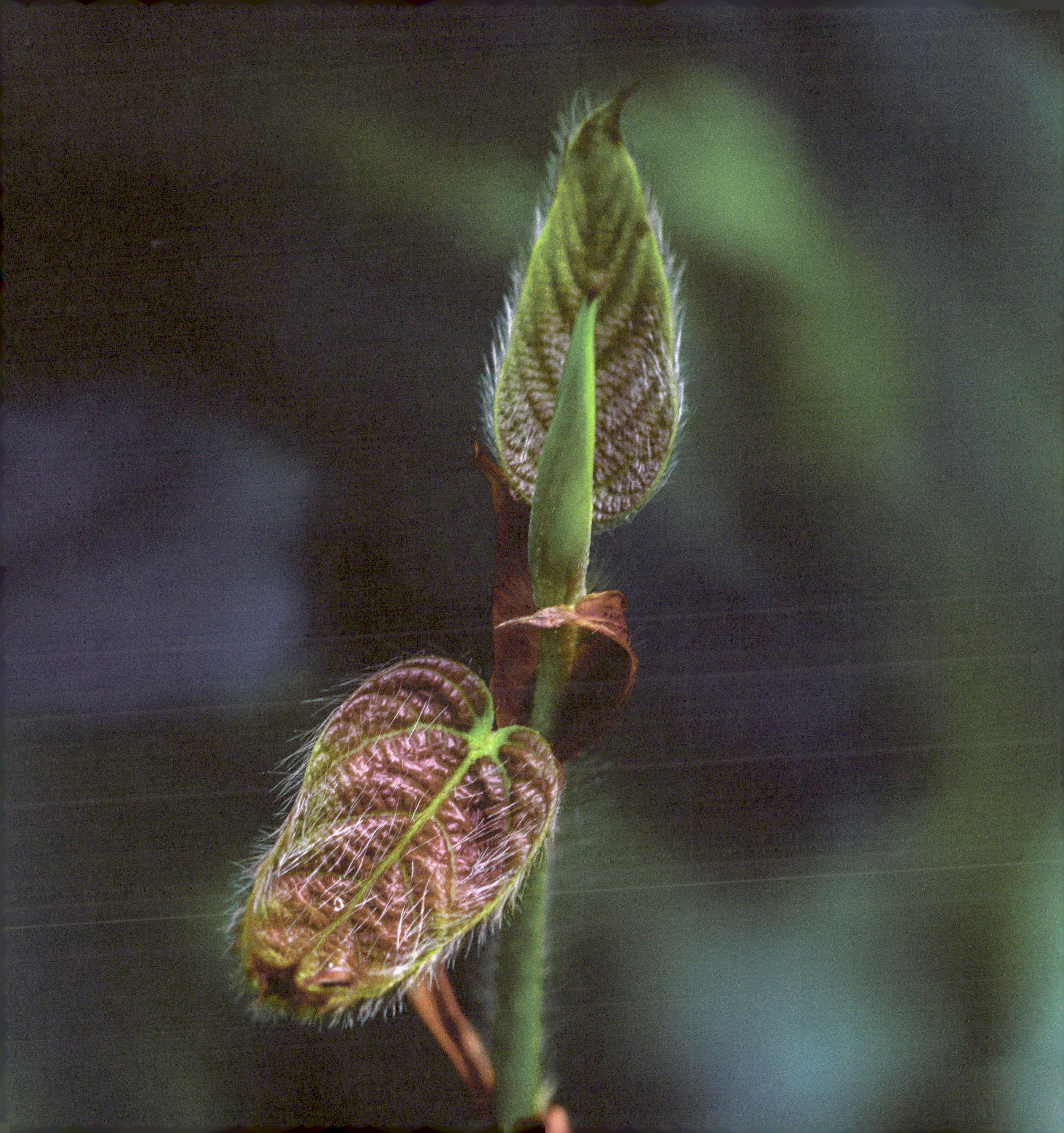

Anger destroys the soul...

Love heals the spirit!

It is hard to stay peaceable when you encounter anger. Anger destroys the peace and harmony of those who cling to it. Walk away and call the angry person to peace with love. Send them light as you keep your loving spirit focused on good. Don't let anyone hinder your loving spirit.

Daily Affirmation

I walk in peace and love today.

Healing Light 2016
Big Bear Lake, CA

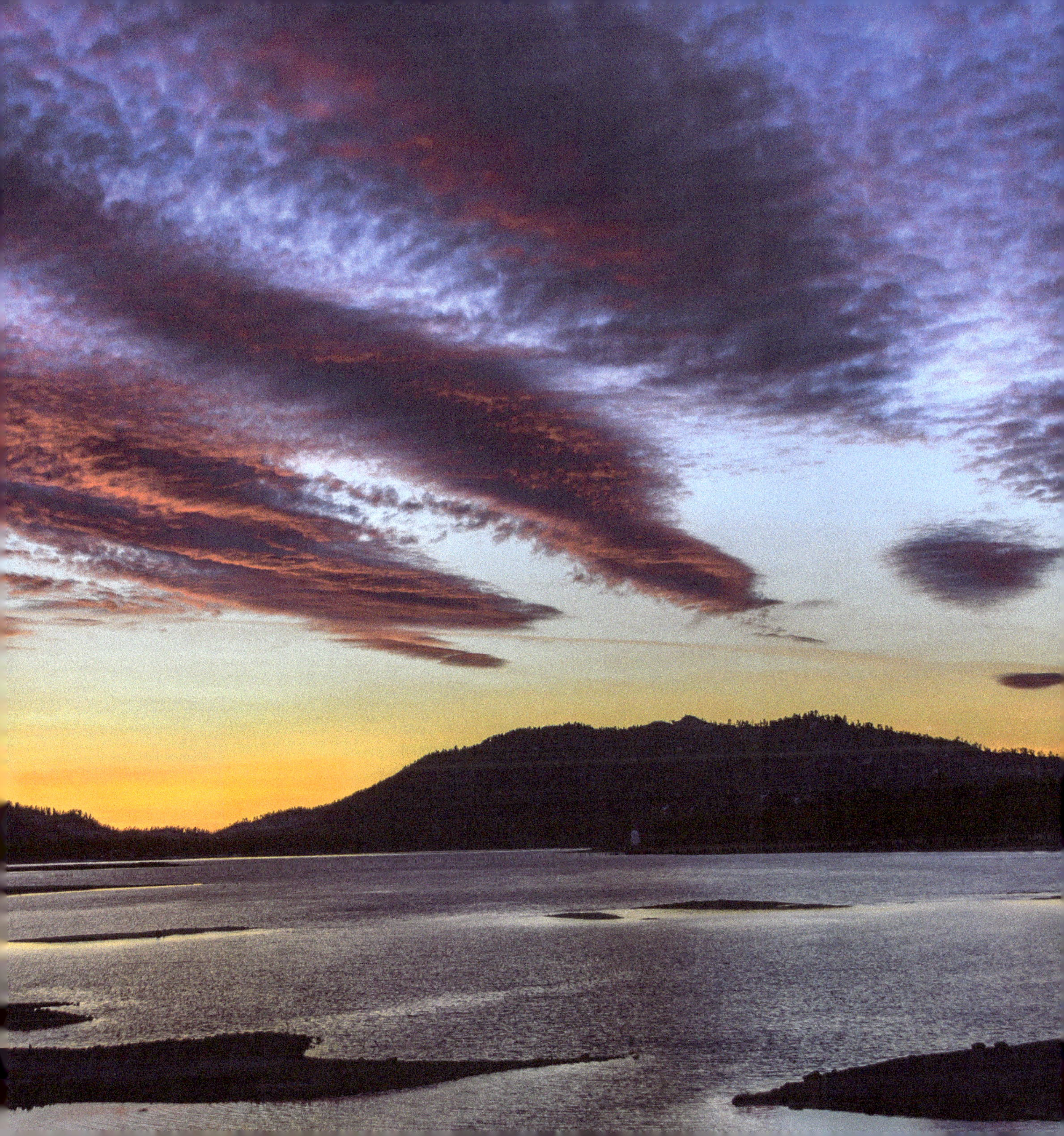

Send love to others…

Embrace the love that comes to you!

The beauty of love comes in a full circle. Love that is sent out from you returns to you. It may not be from the person you expect, but it most definitely will come back to you. Embrace it and be grateful. You are loved!

Daily Affirmation

I embrace the love given to me and send it to others.

Healing Love 2014
Cabo San Lucas, Mexico

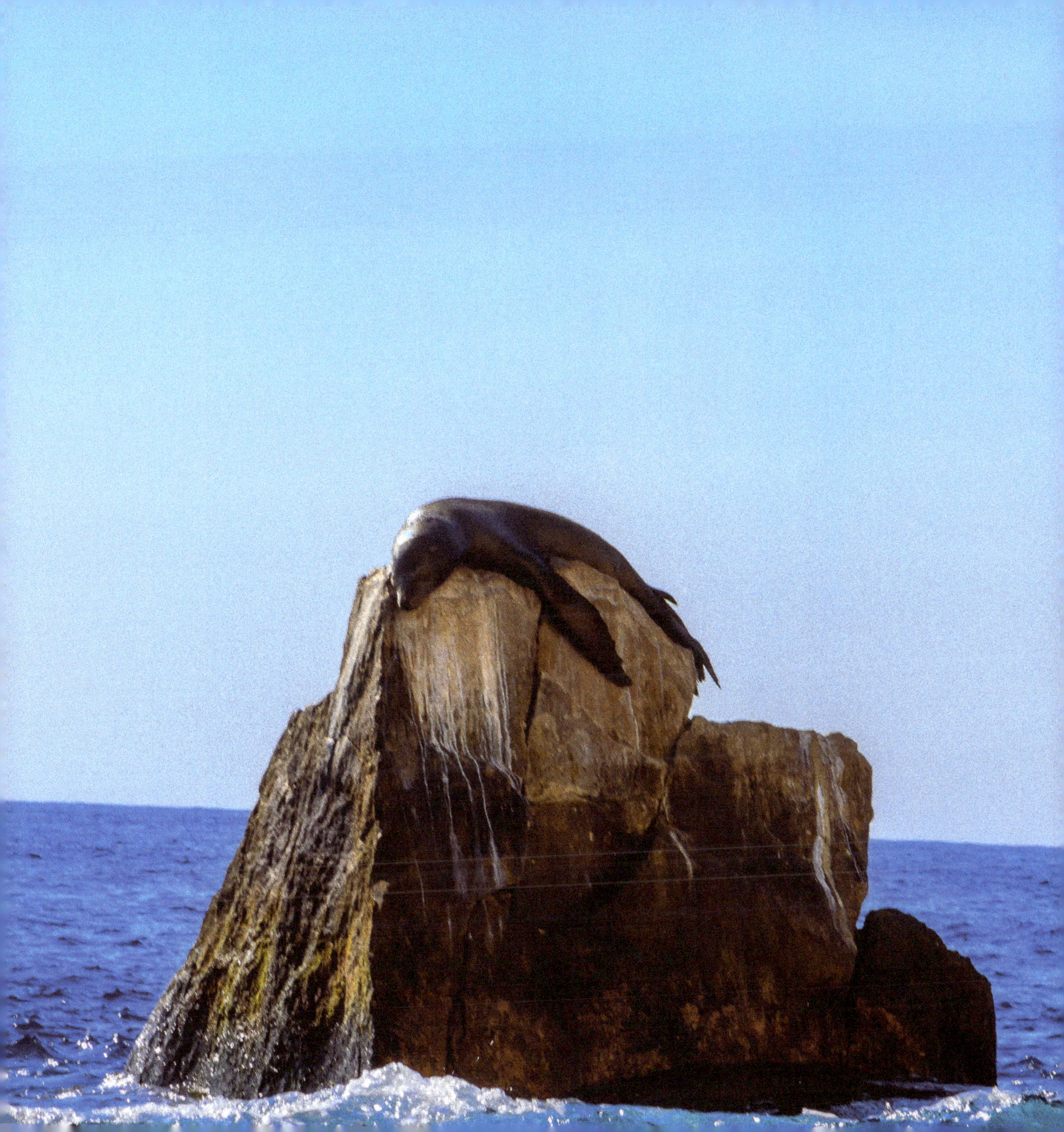

Part III

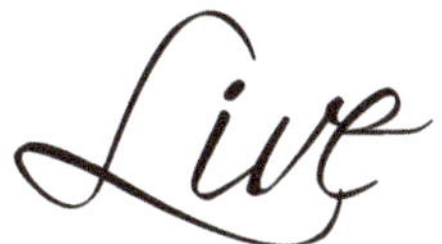

Footsteps slow and mind clear…

I see beauty everywhere!

When you move too fast you may miss what is right in front of you. A busy mind can't see past its own boundaries. Slow down and clear your mind. You will gain focus, clarity, and the ability to see the beauty around you. Bask in the beauty of nature and life.

Daily Affirmation

I am focused and clear. I see beauty everywhere.

Zen Steps 2015
San Marino, CA

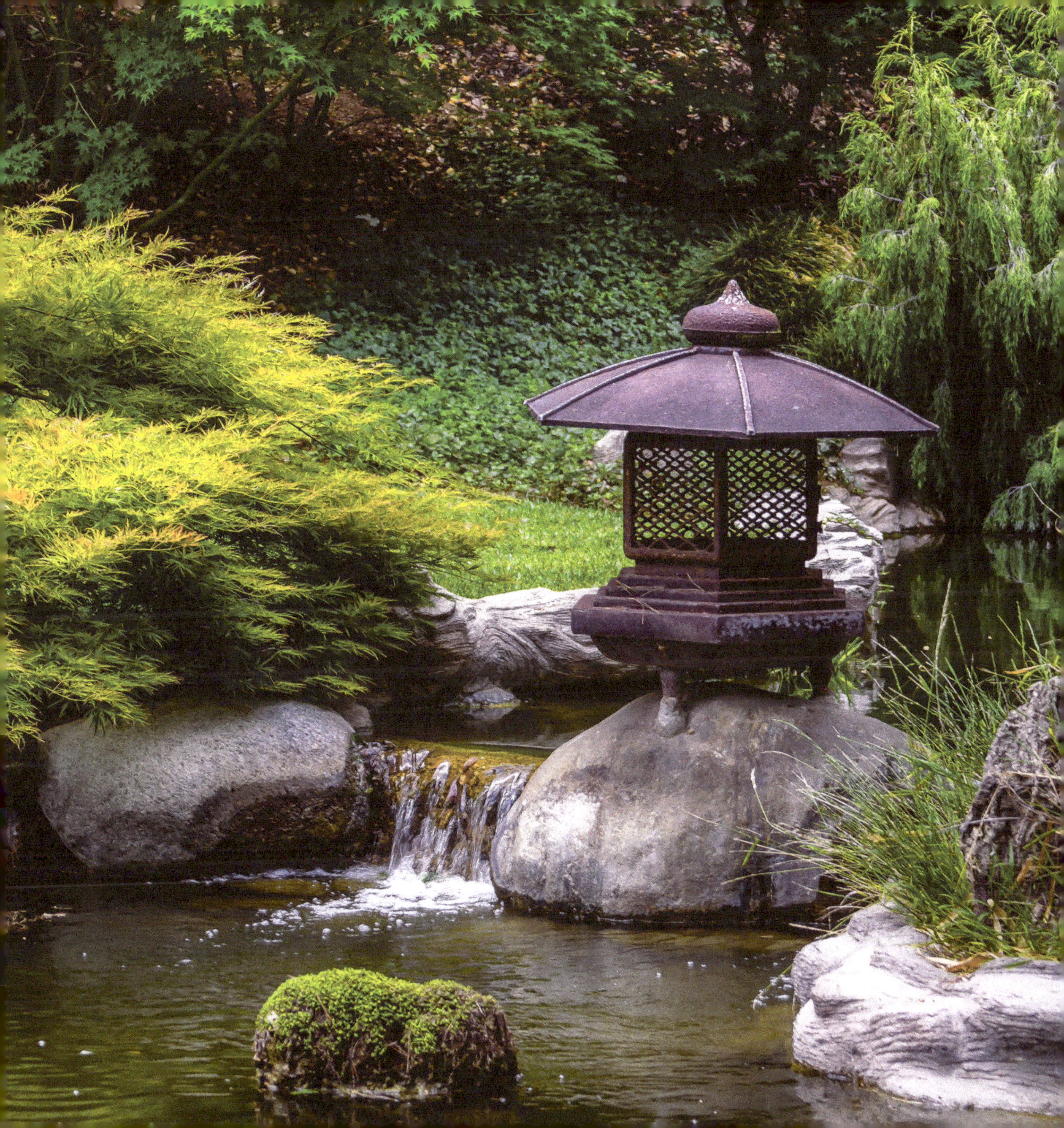

Let the unknown be…

Your path to new beginnings!

Fear can stop you if you allow it. View the unknown as a new possibility and an opportunity for change. What is the worst that could happen? Your plan doesn't work as you anticipated. You tried, it's done, so move on and try something else. Create a pathway of new beginnings.

Daily Affirmation

I am courageous. I embrace something new.

Pathways 2015
Grand Canyon, AZ

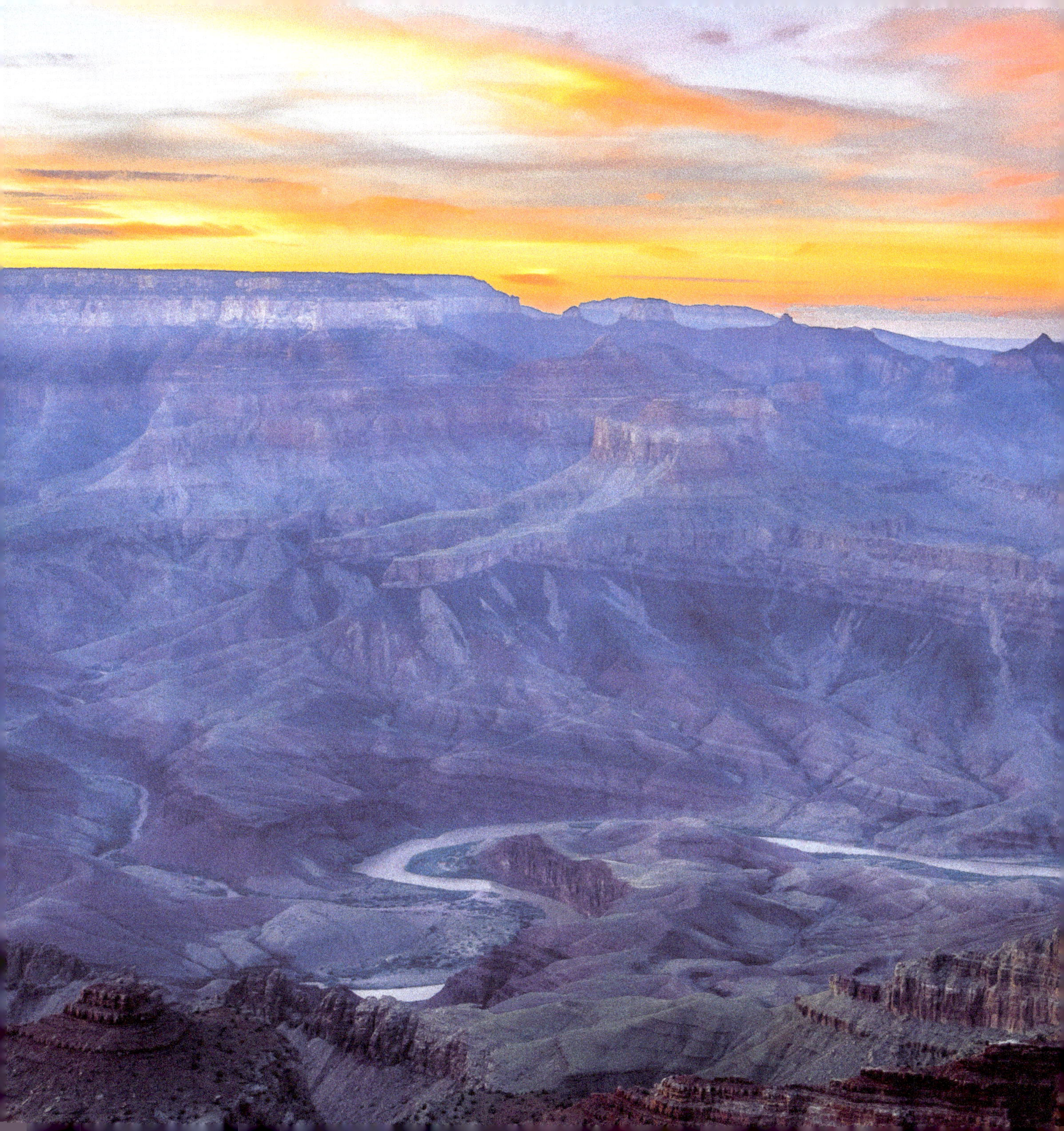

If I lose my way…

I find the light and see clearly!

It is easy to get sidetracked and lose focus. Your perfect plan may be derailed by the pressures of life. Don't become disillusioned. Find your clear path again. Meditate, think positive thoughts, and proclaim positive affirmations daily. Pick yourself up and start again.

Daily Affirmation

Today I am clear and focused.

Dark to Light 2014
Estes Park, CO

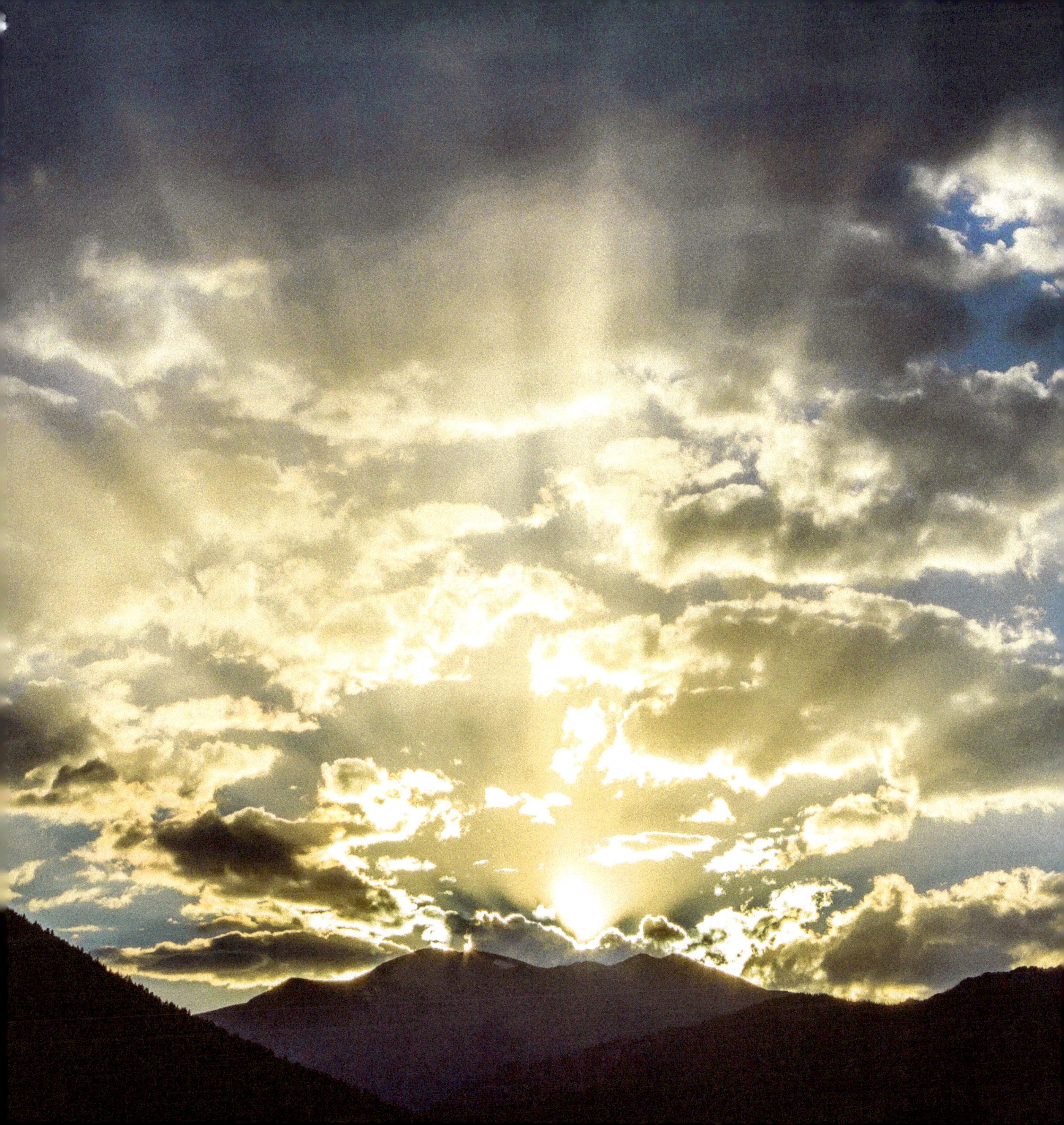

Change your sorrows and regrets…

Into positive life lessons!

No one is immune to the sadness felt from failure or negative life situations. Don't wallow in the sadness. Instead take steps to change the negative into positive. Be forgiving, show empathy, be kind, send love not resentment, learn a life lesson, and be peaceable.

Daily Affirmation

I turn my sadness into life lessons and stepping stones for success.

After the Fog 2014
Grand Canyon, AZ

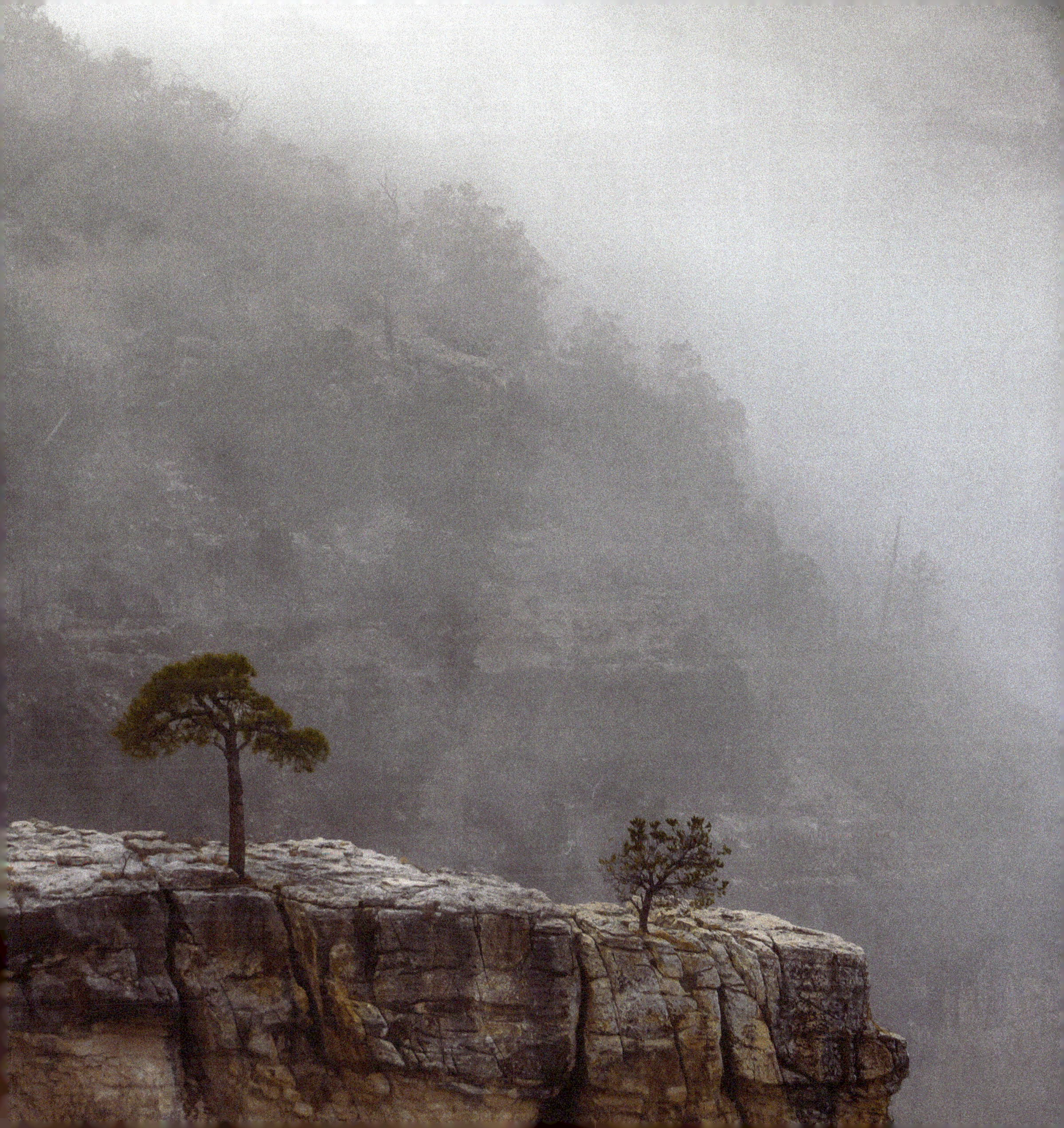

Shadows turn into light…

Light brings clarity and hope!

Don't let the dark shadows from your past hinder you with fear. Refuse to let them cripple you in the present. Let your faith be bigger and stronger than your fears. Learn the life lessons your past provides. Let them fill you with light that brings clarity and hope.

Daily Affirmation

Today fear cannot stop me. I have light and hope.

Sunrise Majesty 2014
Puerto Vallarta, Mexico

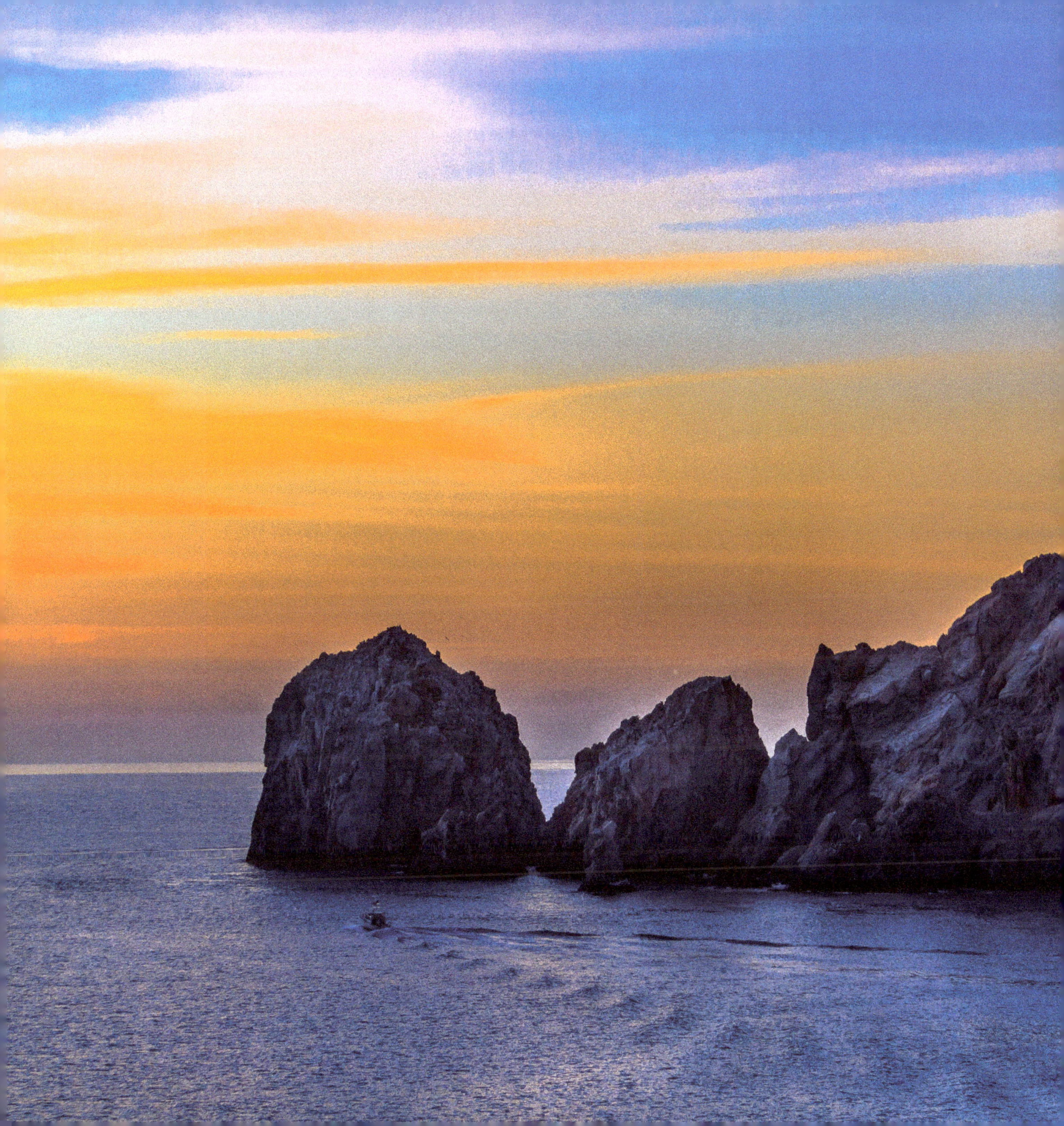

I will start with just one…

Then grow it to abundance!

How do you create abundance? One tree sprouts, grows, drops seeds, then multiplies. Before long a forest is created. One idea, project, goal, or feeling sprouts. Cultivate it, nourish it, nurture it, and watch it grow. This is the key to abundance.

Daily Affirmation

Today I create abundance from what I have right now.

Start with One 2014
Grand Canyon, AZ

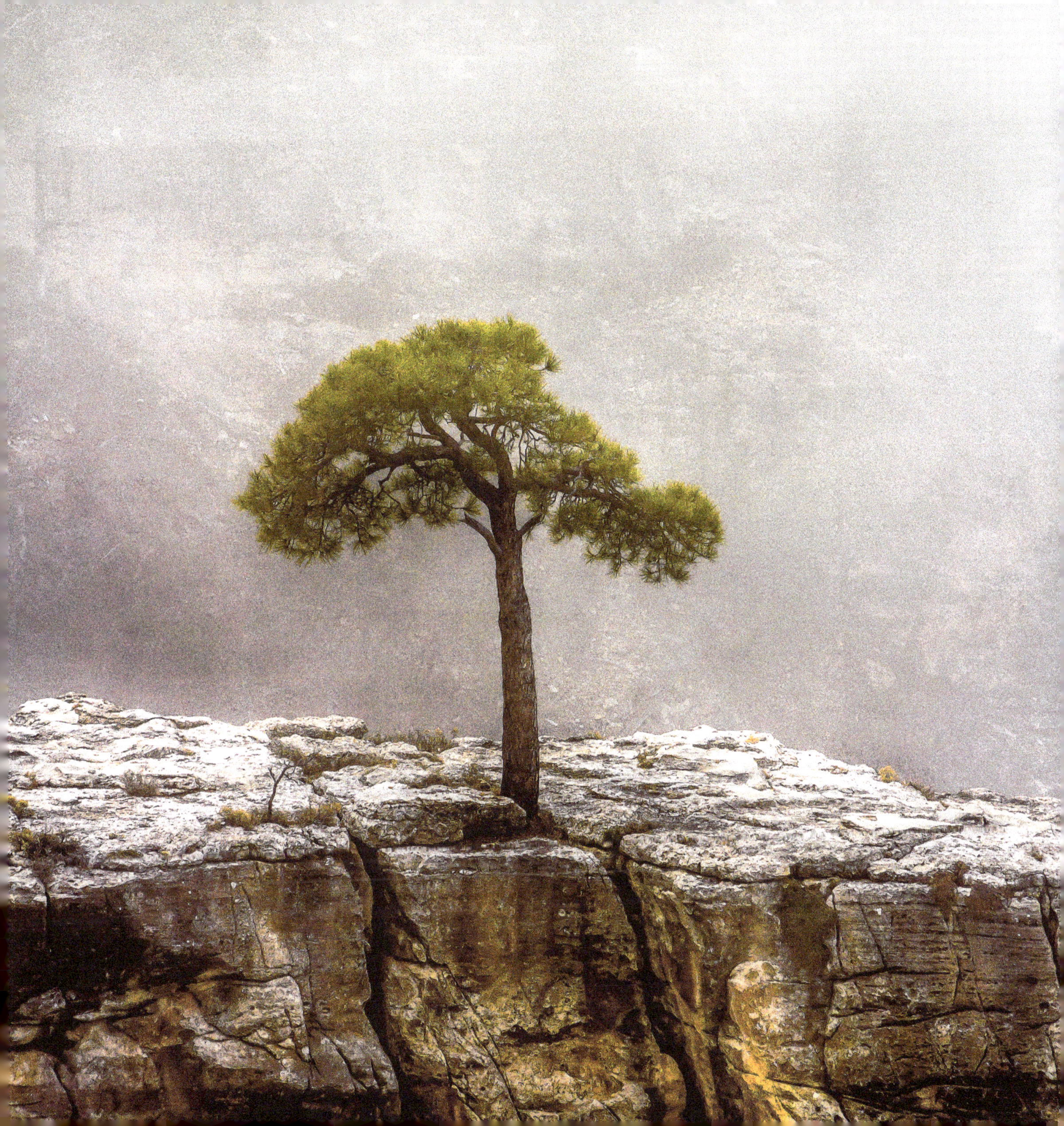

Part IV

Inspire

Breathe in positivity…

Exhale doubts and fears!

The foundation of accomplishment is created by a positive mind and spirit. Cultivate a positive outlook never allowing doubts and fears to stumble you. You will be inspired, unstoppable, and ready to conquer the world.

Daily Affirmation

I am positive and unstoppable.

Doubts and fears have no power over me.

Breathe 2015
San Marino, CA

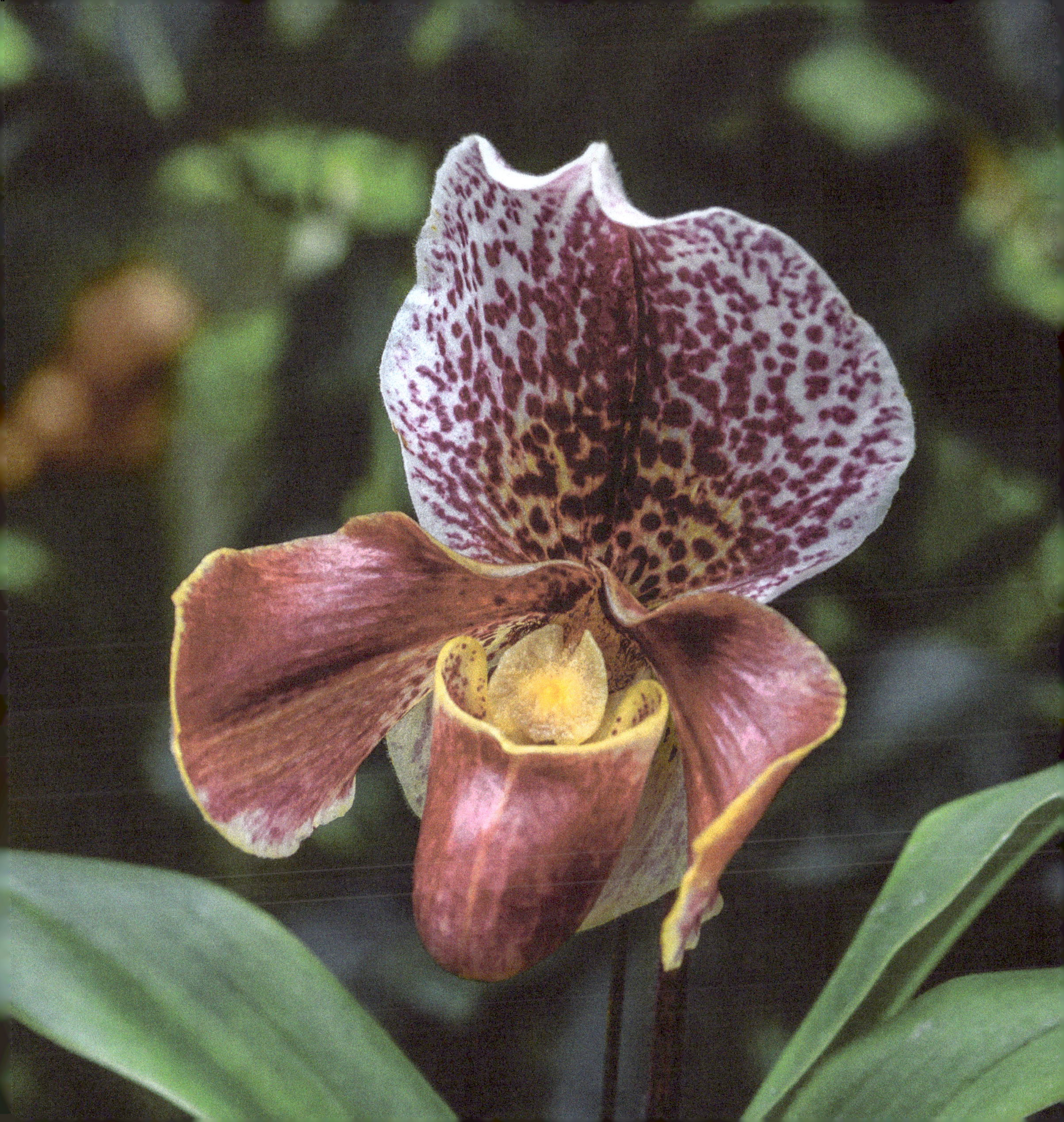

Find your inspiration…

Believe in your dreams!

Every great accomplishment started with an idea or a dream. You are inspired and your passion grows. Passion fuels your positive energy and focus propels your forward. What inspires you? Find your passion, believe in your dreams, and live in your greatness.

Daily Affirmation

I am inspired. I passionately follow my dreams.

Inspired 2013
Moreno Valley, CA

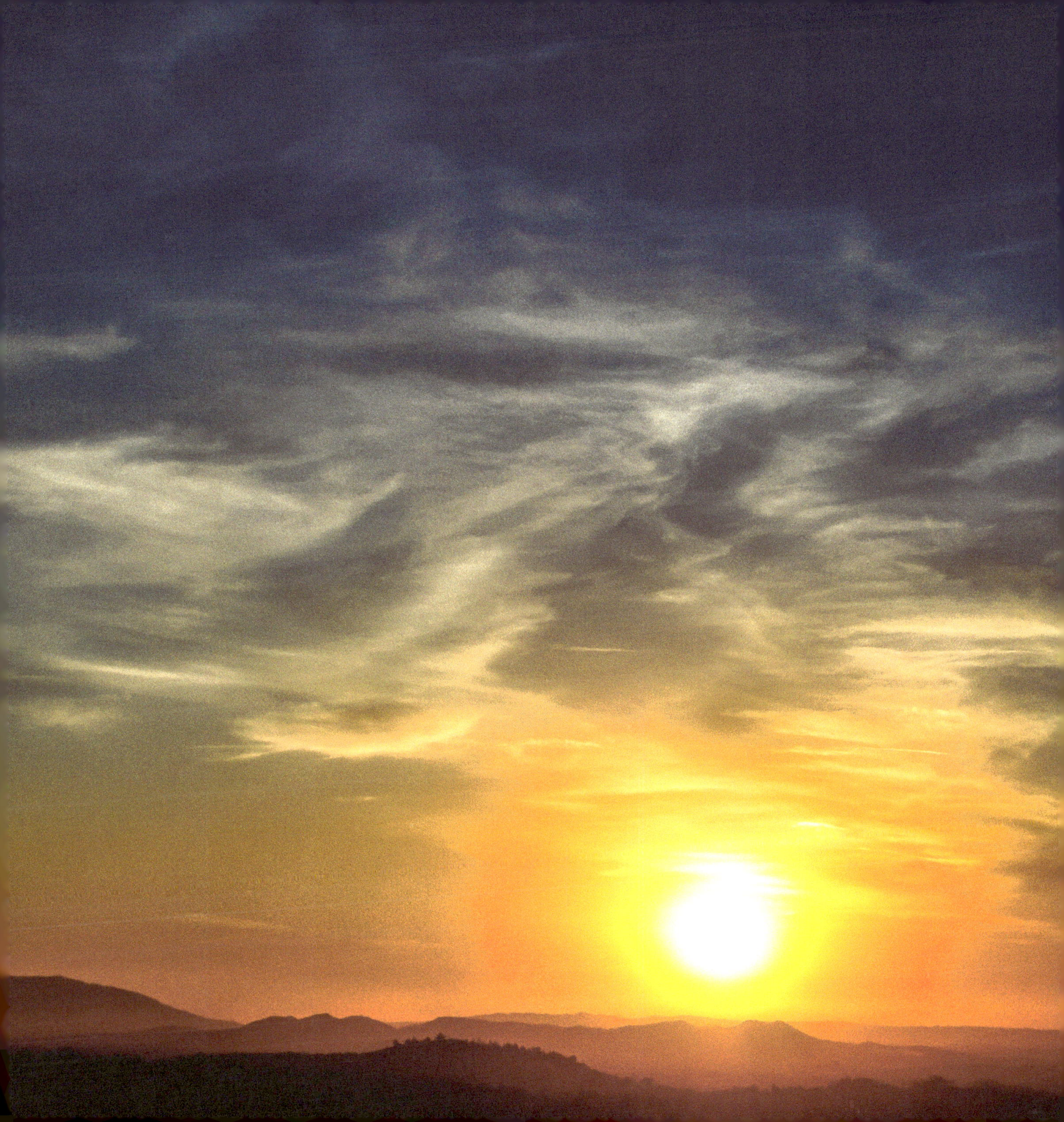

Nature reveals its beauty…

Beauty flows from your heart!

Nature screams loudly "I am magnificent." Do you feel the grandeur and illuminating beauty of the Universe? Be grateful, loving, compassionate, and kind. Cultivate the beauty of your heart like the Universe cultivates the beauty in nature.

Daily Affirmation

I am in awe of the beauty around me, in me, and flowing from me.

Natural Flow 2014
Estes Park, CO

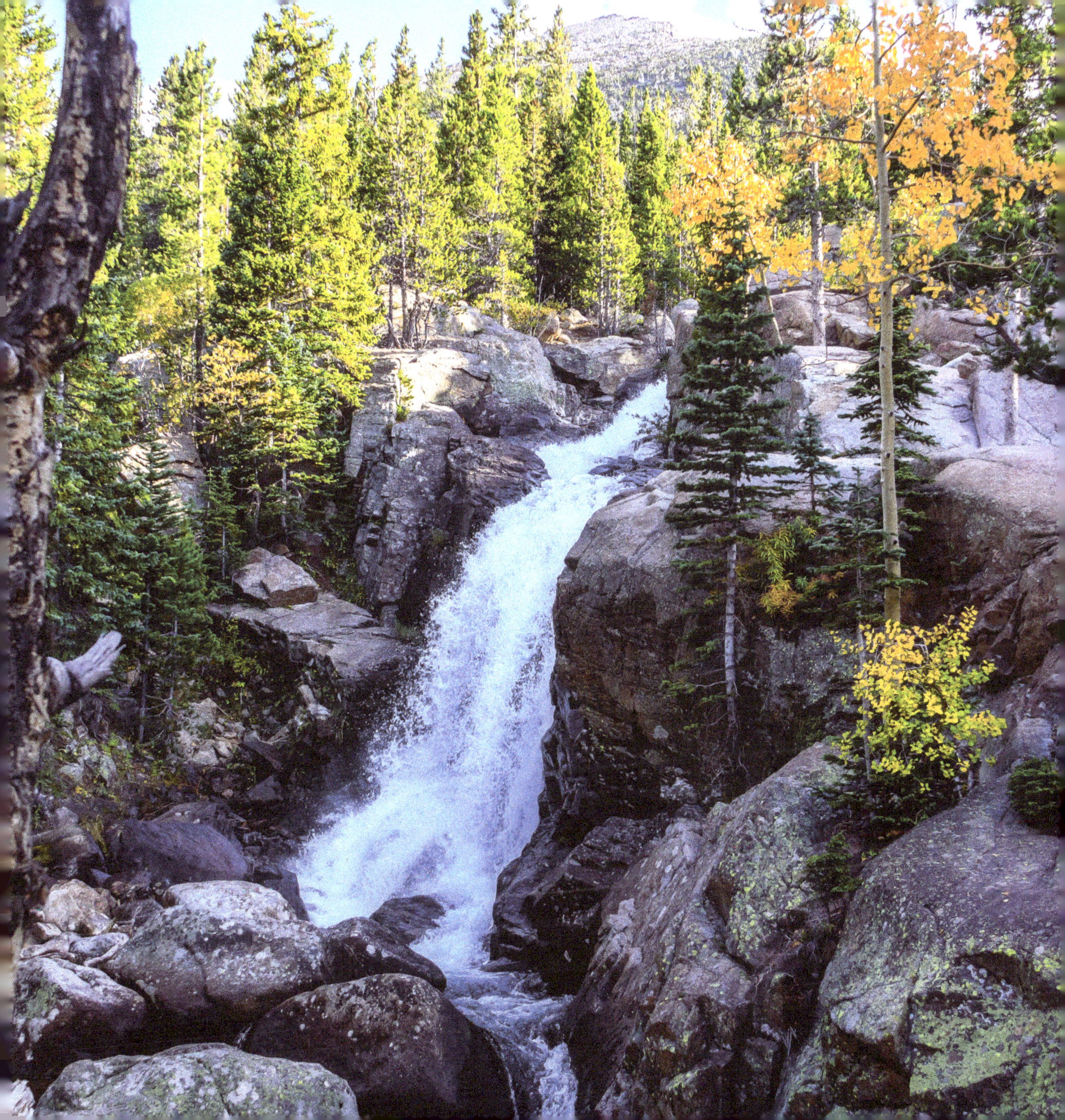

Ignite your inner light…

Illuminate and send it to the world!

Cultivate your heart's inner light. It has been fertilized by life experiences and refined by self-love. Open your heart by filling it with joy, peace, compassion, and love. Send your golden light to others by visualizing it flowing to, around, and through the person you envision.

Daily Affirmation

I am light. I send my light to you and the world.

After the Storm 2015
San Marino, CA

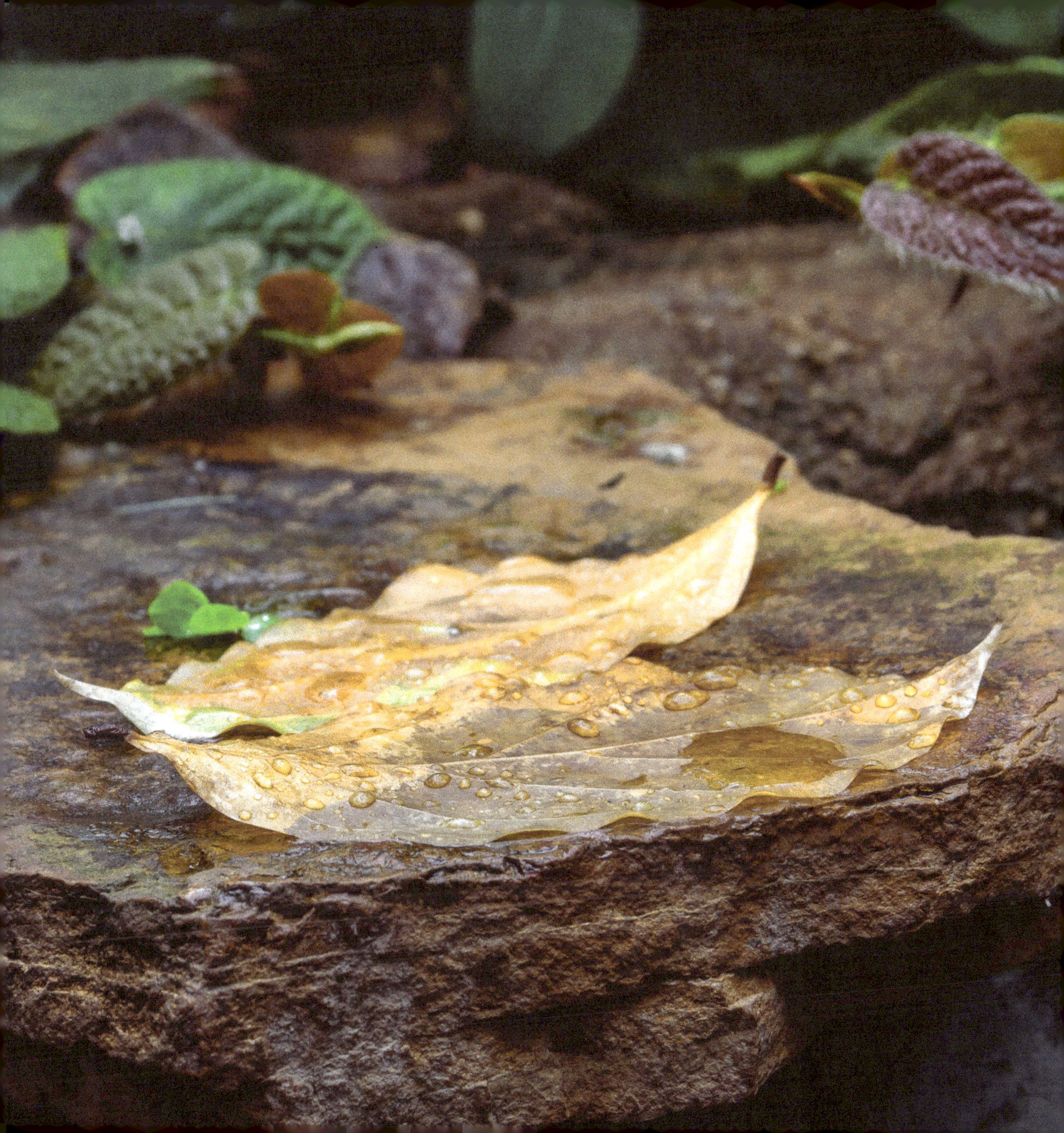

Speak truth with peace in mind...

Hear the words with a loving heart!

Truth comes from light and brings light. It makes things transparent and delightful. Make your truth bring light not harm. Blunt harsh words come from ego. Words spoken with peace bring insight and healing. Speak with love and peace in mind.

Daily Affirmation

I speak truth with peace and love.

Peaceful Heart 2016
Encinitas, CA

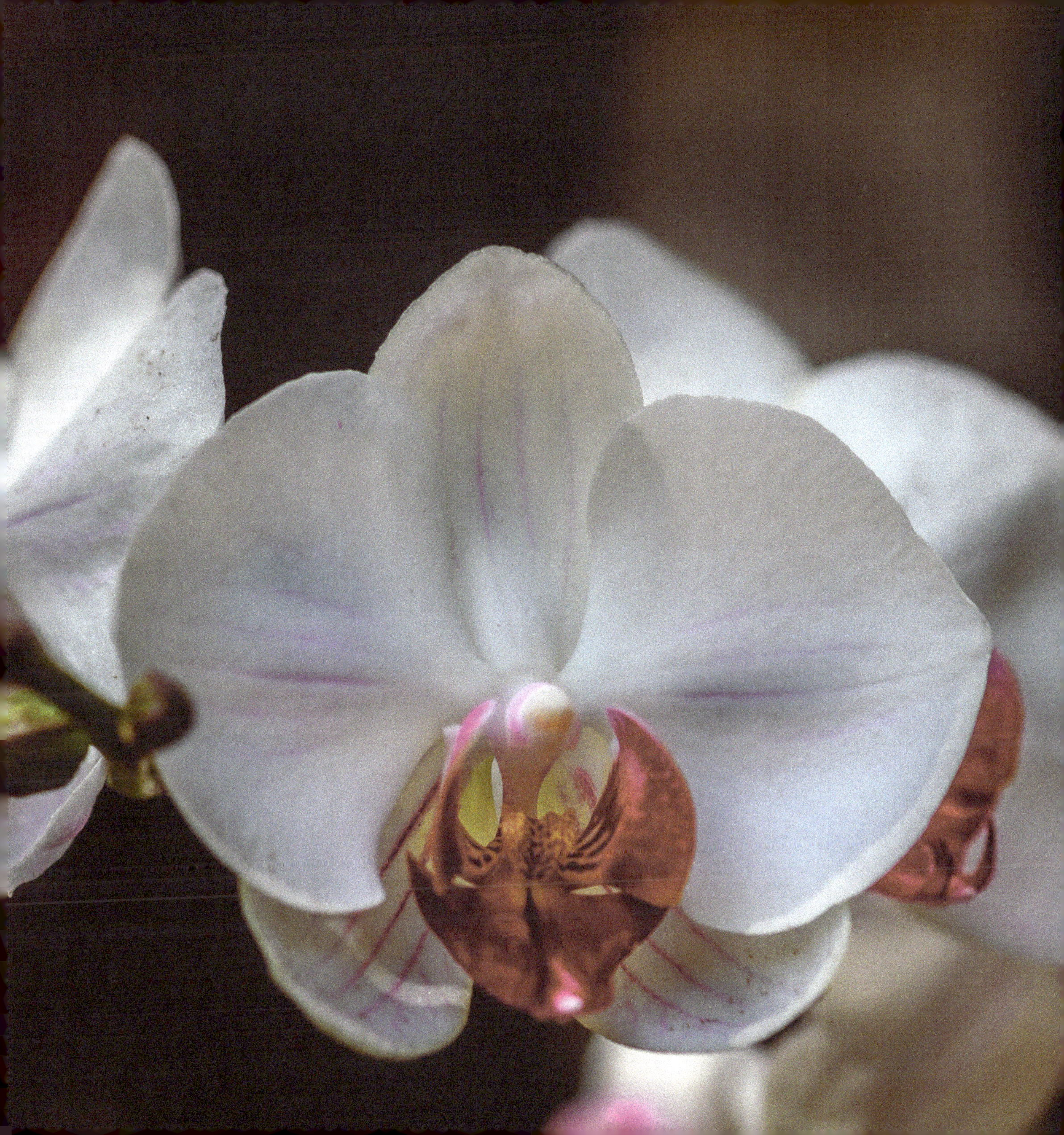

Let go of anger and resentment…

Embrace peace, love, and joy!

Arguments between people cause reactions. Ego says "I am right, how dare you do this to me!" A peaceful heart says "You have your own reality and the right to your opinion." Leave ego behind as you walk away in peace. Send the angry person love with good wishes, without judgement.

Daily Affirmation

I embrace peace and joy. I release all anger and resentment in me.

New Day 2014
Montego Bay, Jamaica

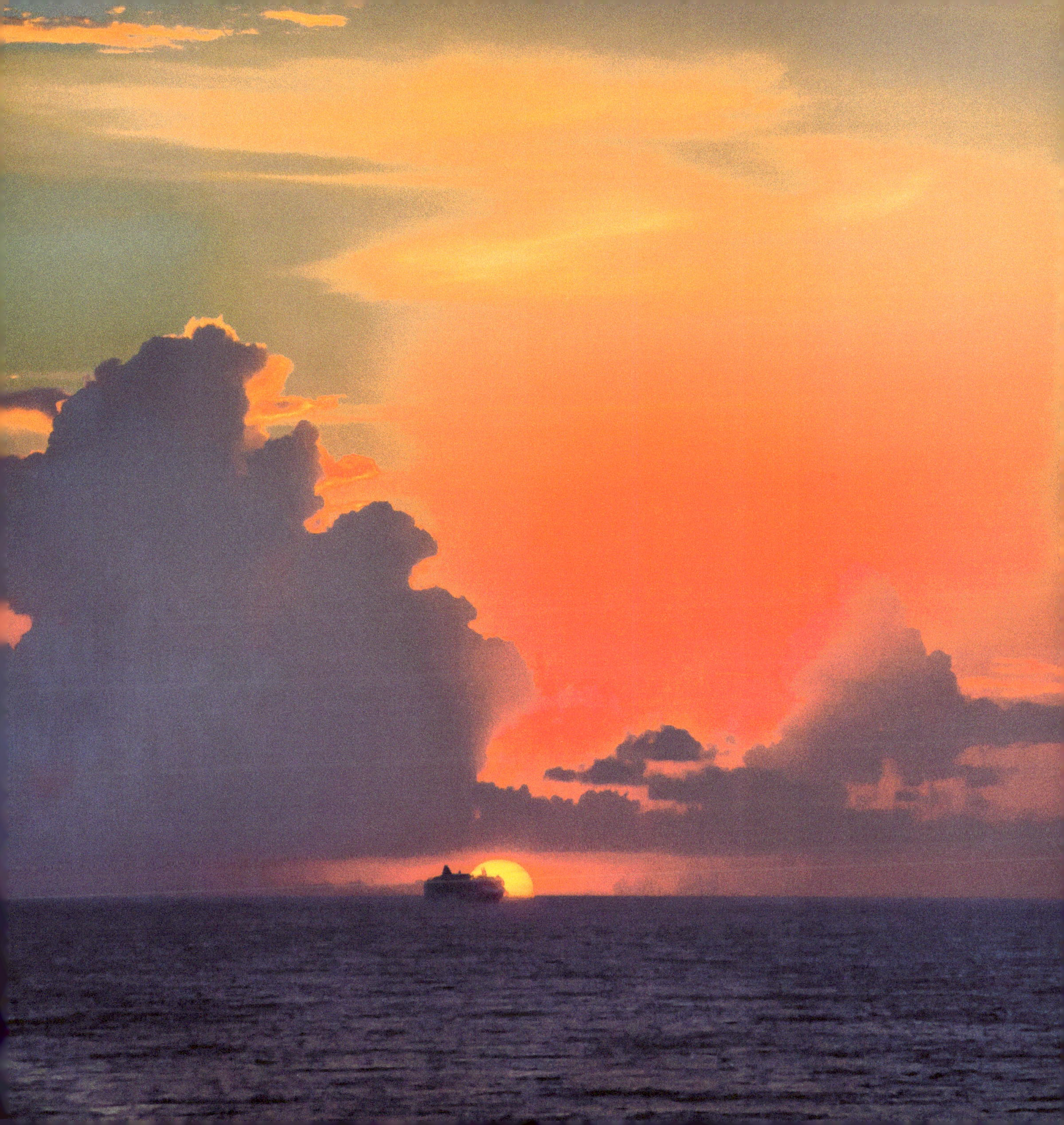

Part V

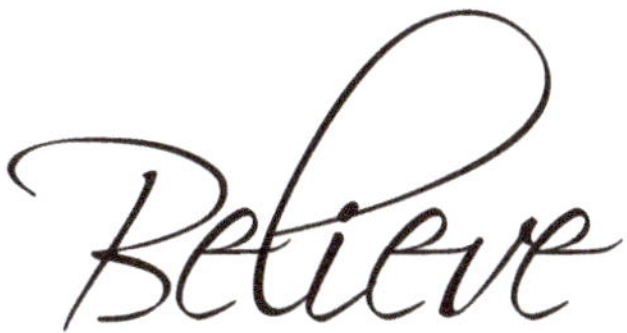

Embrace who you are…

Courageously declare that you are special!

It isn't necessary to be like anyone else. It is vitally important to be yourself. When you are centered and grounded you are living in your truth. Be true to your uniqueness, your heart, and spirit. You will be happy and content as you harmoniously move through life.

Daily Affirmation

I am special. I embrace my uniqueness.

Beautiful Harmony 2016
La Canada, CA

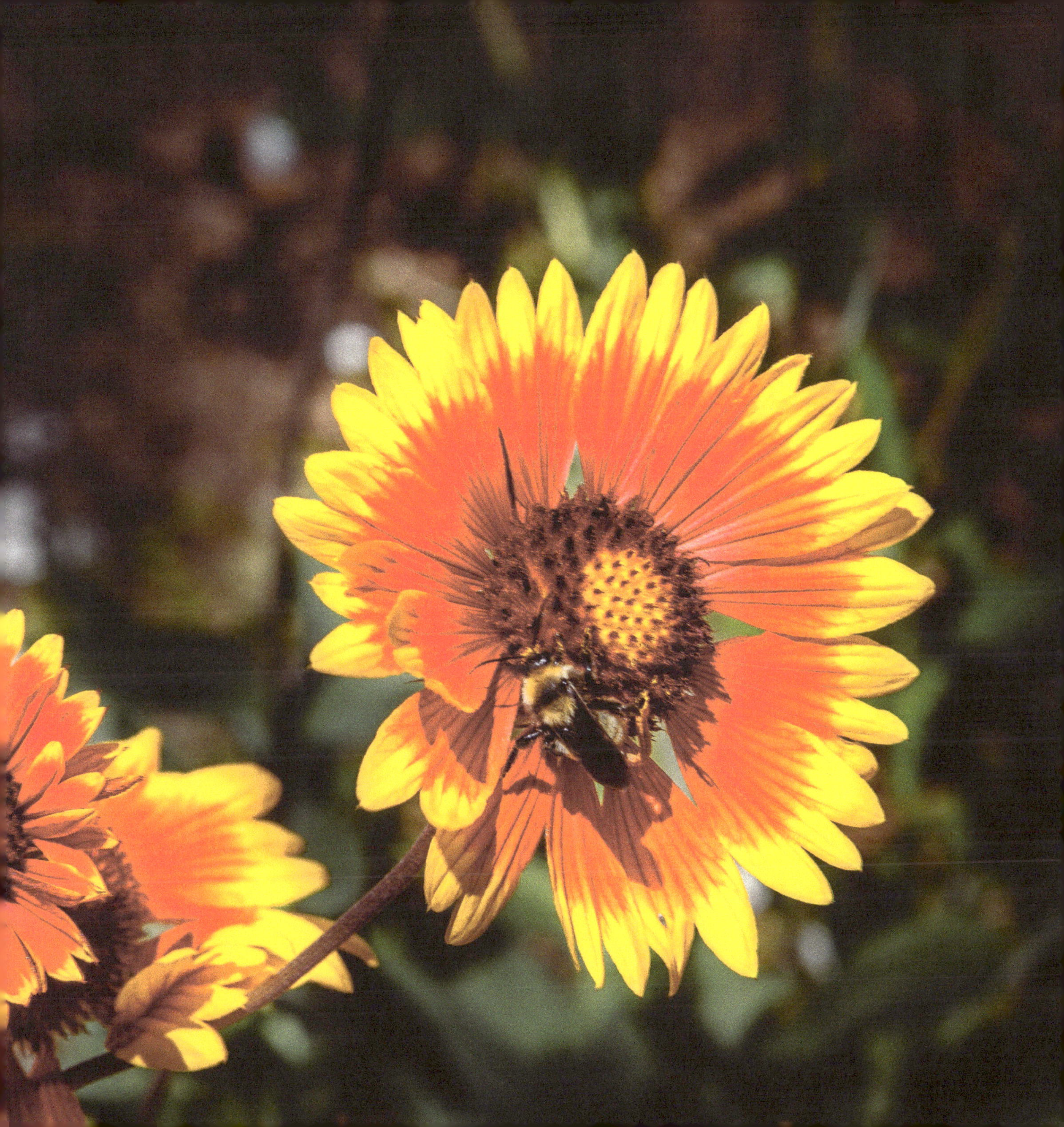

I am powerful…

I achieve whatever I seek to do!

There is nothing that you can't achieve. You are the power behind your greatness and success. Focus on what you want. Keep a positive mind and heart. Declare that it has already happened. Ask, believe, receive…

Daily Affirmation

I am powerful, determined, and unstoppable.

Powerful and Unstoppable 2014
PCH 1, Central Coast, CA

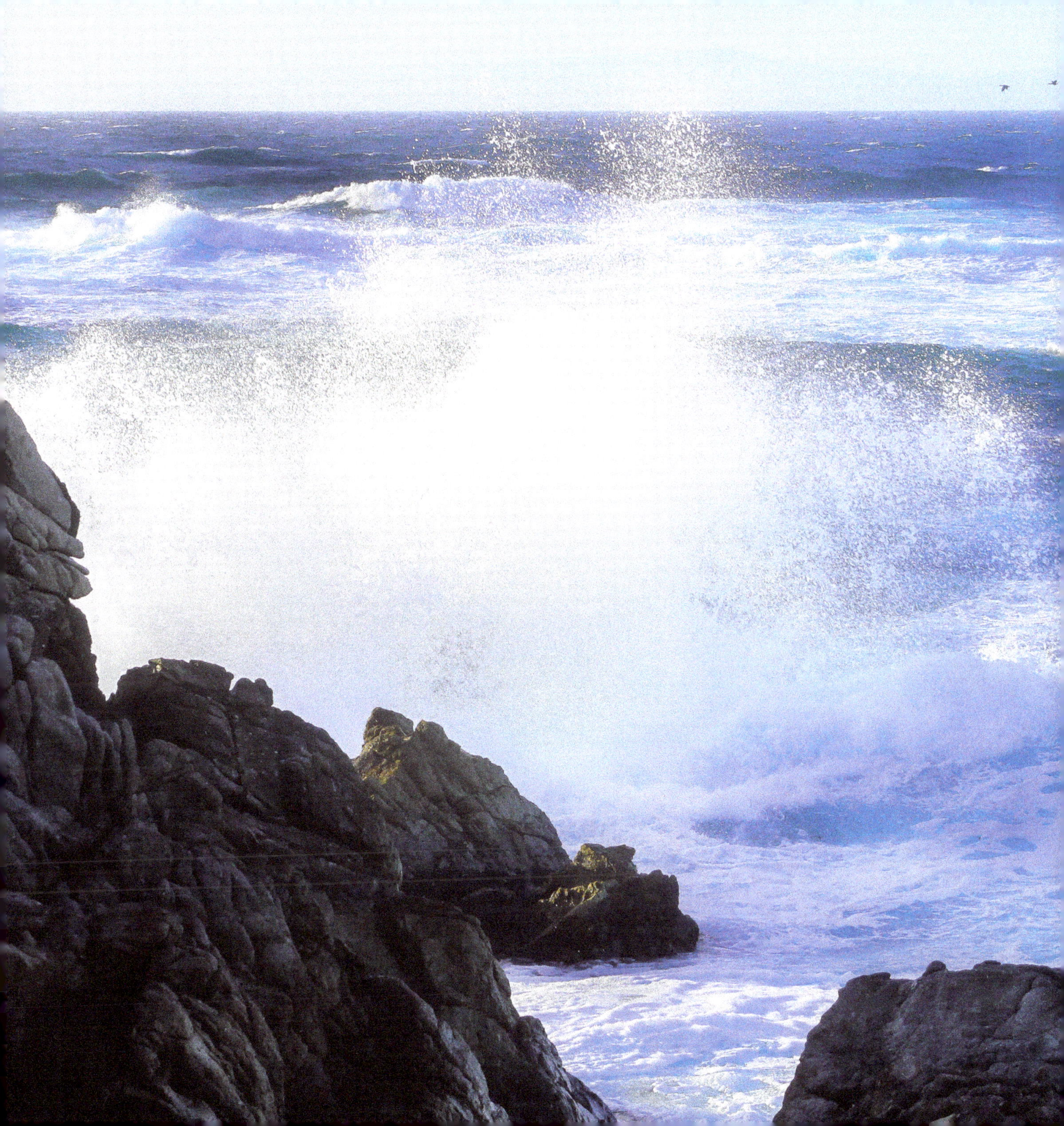

Laugh instead of cry…

A smile is far better than a frown!

Laughter gives you lightness of heart. A smile produces joy and positive energy. Tears sadden the heart. A frown sours the spirit and brings negative energy. Choose the positive pathway to bring all good things to you.

Daily Affirmation

I choose to be happy and positive in all I do.

Simplicity 2016
San Diego, CA

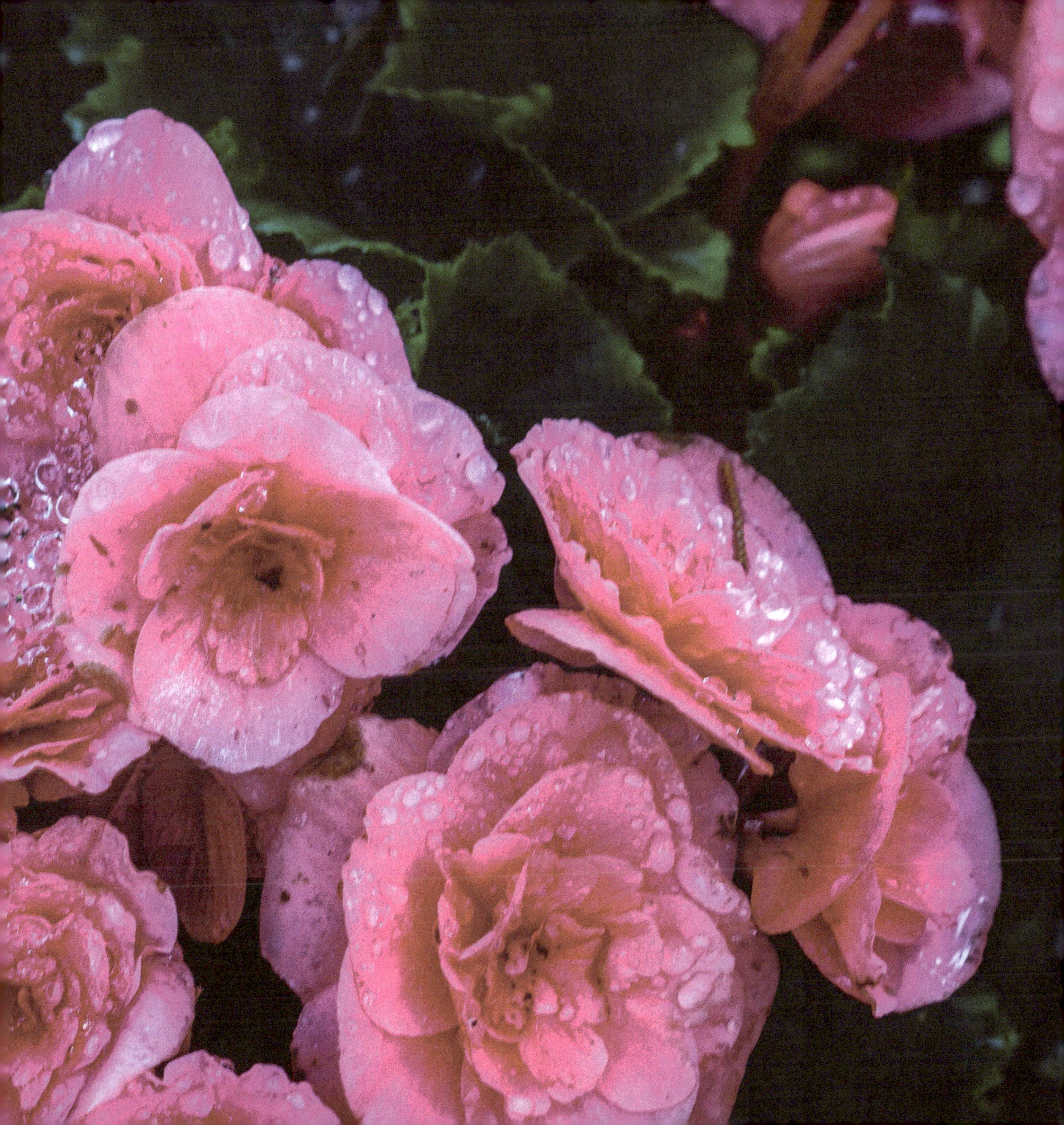

Love yourself enough to say…

I believe I am amazing!

Self-doubts, fear, negativity, and lack of love hold you back and cloud your true potential. A skewed self-image clouds your vision and confidence. Stand up and see the greatness you encompass. Embrace yourself in love and get ready to fly.

Daily Affirmation

I am full of love. I am amazing.

Just Amazing 2016
Big Bear Lake, CA

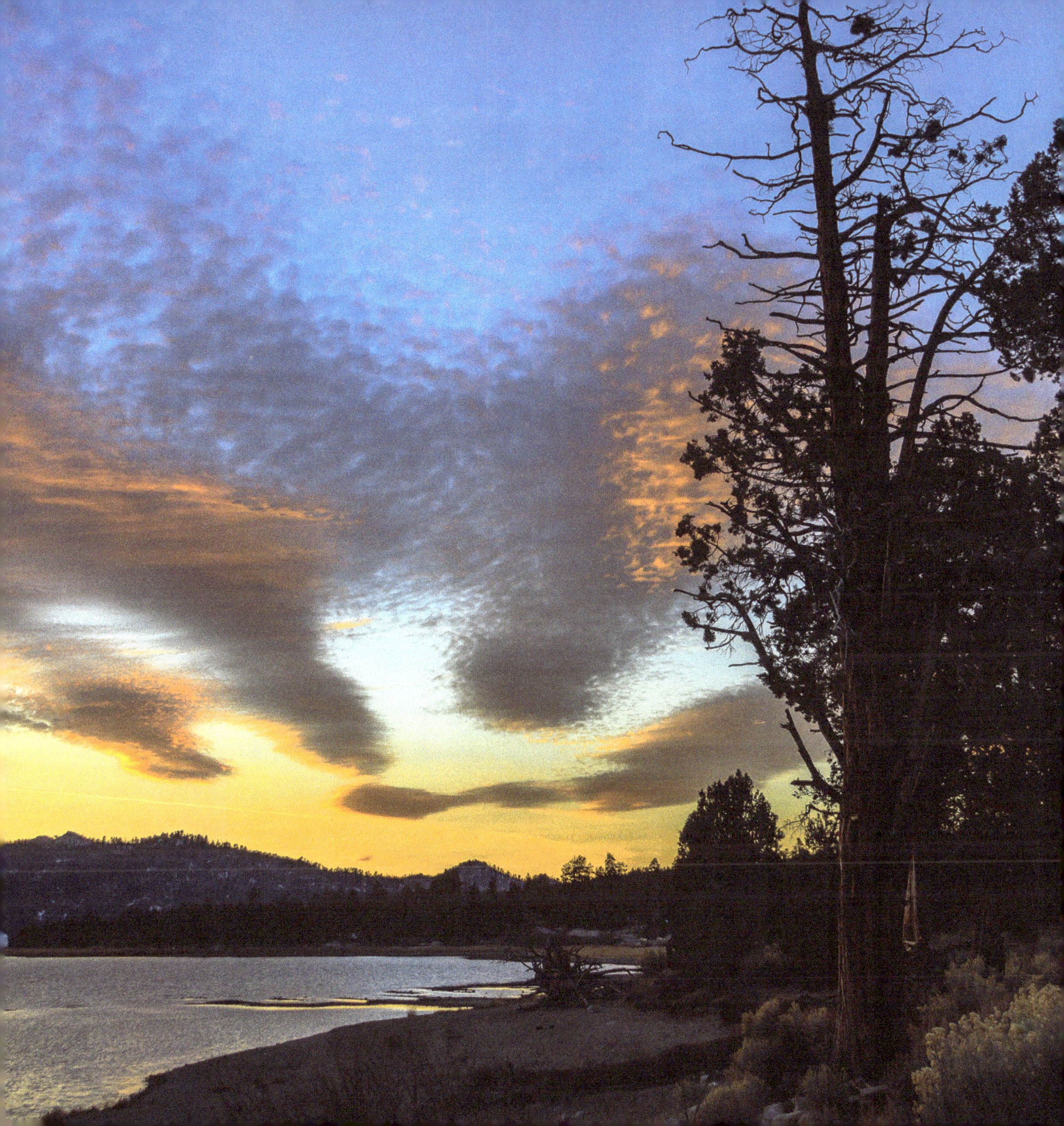

Look into your heart…

Find the secret of life!

Our grand universe whispers the secrets and truth about life. You hold the greatest treasure of all…your heart center of love! All good things spring from love. Use your love to light up the world.

Daily Affirmation

I am love. I am truth.

Secret of Life 2013
San Juan Capistrano, CA

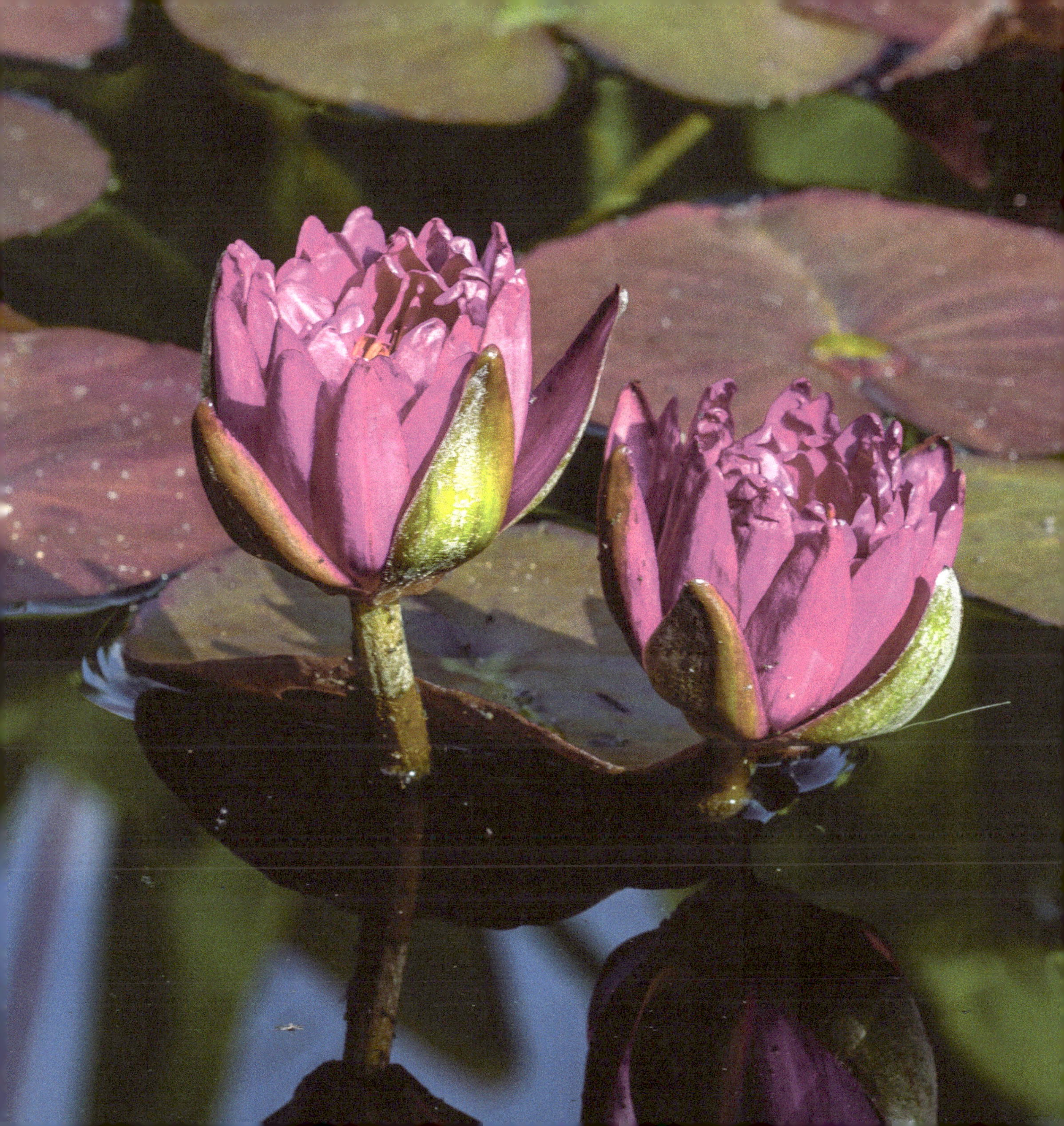

Believe in good…

Look for good!

Your view of the world will influence what you think, what you do, and the results you get. Believe in good and you will find it. See the world with positive eyes and you will experience it. Believe life is against you and so it will be. Be wise and believe in good.

Daily Affirmation

I believe in good in myself and others.

Believe 2016
La Canada, CA

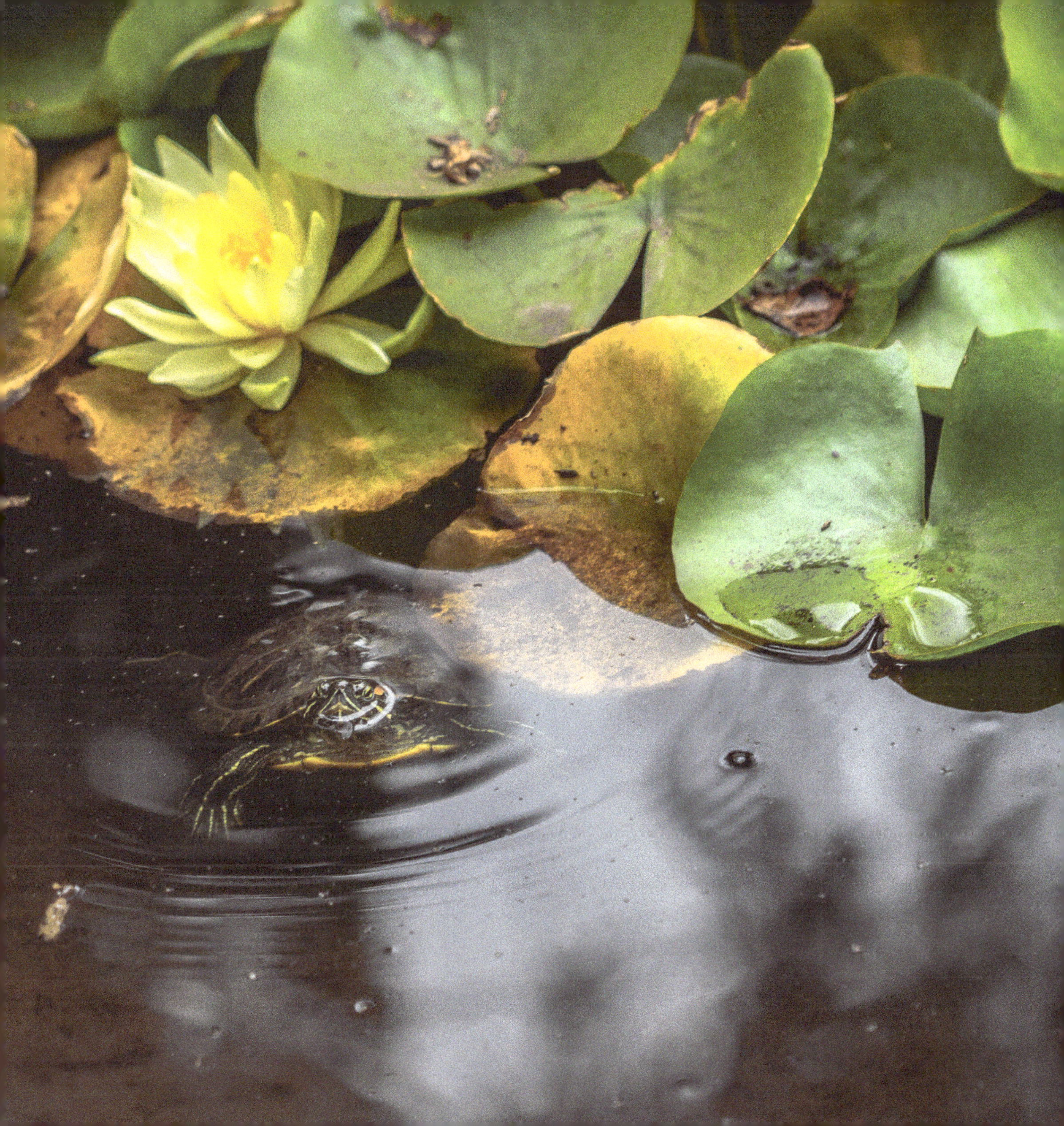

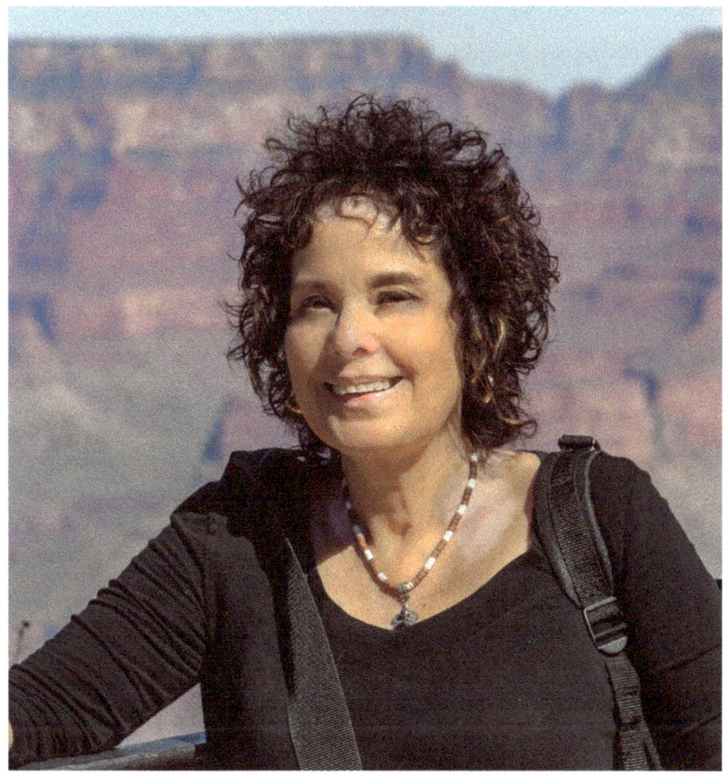

About the Author

Linda Anne is an author, photographer, transformational speaker, educator, mother, grandmother, and lover of light and truth. She has written three books: *The Voice Hidden Within Me*, *Simply Tasty – Easy Meals on a Budget*, and her new book *Light to Your Heart*. Each book is different but yet connected by her intention to inspire the reader to live a joy-filled healthy life.

Linda Anne is passionate about travel, photography, and cultivating a spirit of peace, love, and joy. She brings you experiences gleaned from her own life lessons and her travel across the globe. Her mantra is live in truth, be yourself, and spread your light to others.

To learn more, visit www.HeartChatter.com

www.ingramcontent.com/pod-product-compliance
Lightning Source LLC
LaVergne TN
LVHW060641110826
845147LV00018B/1020
* 9 7 8 0 9 8 8 5 4 5 3 5 9 *